Memories of a 99 Year Old Lady

Vera B. Reed

Copyright © 2013 Vera B. Reed
All rights reserved.

ISBN-13: 9781493762675
ISBN-10: 1493762672

I am dedicating this book to Quinton and Mary Helen who have helped me in so many ways to stay independent and live in my home.

The steps of a good man are ordered by the Lord: and he delighteth in his way. Psalm 37:23

Chapter 1

My mother and father were raised on farms separated by a fence and they talked over the fence all their young days. When they were teenagers they realized they were in love with one another, so they married. Dad took Mother to live in the house next to the country store he owned. Almost four years later I was born during the depression and they named me Vera Beulah. There was a midwife attended to my birth, at which time she declared.

"Oh! There is a veil over this baby's face." The Spirit of the Lord moved upon the midwife and she gave a prophecy concerning her future.

"God has His hand on this baby and she will reach and win souls for the Lord." My mother didn't tell me this prophecy until she was 89 years old, during the time she was in my home after having a pacemaker put in to control her heart beat.

During the depression people lost their jobs and were unable to pay their bill at my father's store. After a period of running a successful business, he realized he would have to go out of business. My mother's sister, Aunt Flora and her husband Uncle Phillip, came to Virginia to take his wife back to a coal mining town in Wilcoe, West Virginia. Uncle Phillip encouraged my father to go back to Wilcoe, with his wife and family, where there were many jobs available. Father got a job loading coal in the mines. After that, the first thing he did was to rent a house and return home to move Mother, myself and my sister Lena, who was thirteen months younger than me, to our new home in Wilcoe. All homes in Wilcoe were double houses. They were laid off in blocks with alleys between each row. All homes were made with good materials, hardwood floors, plaster walls and good woodwork. All the rooms were large and the living room, dining room and two upstairs bedrooms had fireplaces where we burned coal and they had tall removable screens in front to keep sparks from flying.

Shortly after we moved in, my mother warned me not to go downstairs by myself. My sister Lena, six months old, was asleep on the bed. Mother covered her with my father's coat before going downstairs. I was sitting on the floor in front of the tall fireplace screen, playing with my dolls, when I looked up and saw fire on the bed. I knew it wasn't supposed to be there. I jumped up and ran to the top of the stairs and screamed as loud as I could.

"Mother, Eeny on fire! Eeny on fire!" When she didn't answer, I screamed again jumping up and down full of panic. Finally, Mother heard me and she ran up the steps, quick as possible, and put out the fire. Lena was burned on the lower part of her right cheek and on her little arm. I was heartbroken and cried and cried. *The strange thing was we never knew where my sister got the open box of matches lying on her bed. She either got them out of father's coat pocket or the matches fell out of the coat when mother draped it over her.*

To add to the excitement of our family, a few months later, Mother gave us another sister, Alma. When I was three or four years old I was out playing on the front lawn, which was fenced. There was a mound of dirt, which was a perfect rectangle. It was about two feet long and about thirteen inches wide. The grass on that mound was different from the surrounding grass. It was soft, with no weeds, and I ran my hand over it and then I wanted to feel it on my bare feet. When I stepped my foot on the top of the mound my heel landed on a sewing needle. The needle went so far up in my heel that my mother couldn't pull it out. At that moment a man, named Mr. Sparks, came along and saw the commotion. When he saw the needle he knew he would not be able to pull it out with his fingers either. He went back to his home, which was next door to ours, and brought back tweezers to extract the needle.

Mr. and Mrs. McGee lived in the double house with us and they didn't have any children. Mrs. McGee took a fancy to me and took me to her house for chocolates from a box that her husband had bought for her. Mr. McGee worked at night and slept during the day. One morning Mother bathed me and dressed me and sat me on the front porch in a rocking chair. Of course, I got restless and got out of my chair and went around to Mrs. McGee's front door. I reached up on my tip-toes. I opened the screen door and stepped into the living room. I stood there calling for her. Finally, I looked around in the living room and saw a box of what I thought was chocolates. I didn't know it was what they called 'fly dope', to attract flies. When the flies ate the sweet chocolates they passed out. Temptation got the best of me and I helped myself to what I thought was candy. I immediately got sick and went out on their front porch and climbed up in their porch swing and laid down. When mother found me I was unconscious and she called Mrs. McGee. When Mrs. McGee saw the chocolate on my mouth she knew that I had eaten 'fly dope'. She began screaming for Mr. McGee as she went upstairs to get him out of bed. He came running out the front door half-dressed and grabbed me in his arms and began running. His intention was to run with me, in his arms about two miles, to the doctor's office. When he reached the front gate, a taxi was there and the driver had already opened the car door for us. I was told he drove recklessly to get to the hospital. *I have often wondered where the taxi and driver came from, since this was the coal fields in about 1917. There were no phones and very few cars.*

The first thing I remember, after eating the 'fly dope', was awakening in the hospital. To my surprise people had shown their sympathy for me and my family by dropping coins and bills on my bed.

I was grieved the day the McGees moved because they were good to me. However, when Mr. and Mrs. Pearson moved in the McGee's house I was pleased that Mrs. Pearson, also took a fancy to me because she had no children.

One day I picked up the broom to sweep the kitchen floor. Baby Alma grabbed the broom out of my hand. When I took it from her, she became angry and picked up a fork and stabbed the top of my left hand with the prongs so deep that Mother couldn't pull it out. Mother ran to the Pearson's house. Mrs. Pearson was a registered nurse. She extracted the fork and treated my hand. I loved Mrs. Pearson because she petted me so much. She took me to her home while her husband was at work. One day she came up our back steps carrying a stew cup. She said, "Would you like to have some tommy toes?"

"What are those?"

"Come with me to my garden and I'll show you what tommy toes are." She and Mother laughed because mother knew what they were.

When we got to the garden, there were tiny red shiny tomatoes in bunches on the tomato vines all over the ground. When I took the stew cup of tommy toes back to Mother she washed them and cut those little small things in half and salted them. We had hot cornbread with buttermilk and tommy toes for lunch. I enjoyed it very much.

Mrs. Pearson and my mother became very close friends and they both made an appointment with the same dentist in Welch. My mother got all dressed up in a beautiful dark blue suit with a georgette silk blouse, which had small shiny beads sewed in rows on the collar. She had on a dark blue hat, which had a small brim across the front and lined with bright pink satin that lit up her face. I thought she was the most beautiful Mother in the whole world. The added touch to her outfit was the elegant wide mink stole my father had bought Mother for Christmas, and the birth of his first born son, Otie Alvis, Jr., that December. However, when Mother opened the door to go out of the house to meet Mrs. Pearson, the three month old baby brother was sitting on my Father's lap. He let out a loud bloodcurdling scream. He never cried much anyway but this scream was so different. The scream was so weird it brought cold chills over my seven-year-old body. My parents thought a pin might be sticking him. Mother checked him and found nothing wrong. She then went to the kitchen and took a soft cloth and added about two tablespoons of sugar to the cloth. She brought the ends of the cloth together and tied it, which in those days was called a 'sugar tit'. While sitting on my Father's lap, Mother tried to put it in Otie's mouth. He totally rejected the 'sugar tit'. Then Mother started out the open door again and Otie let out that bloodcurdling scream again. When Mrs. Pearson came to the door Mother had to tell her.

"I cannot leave my baby screaming like that. It is too unusual."

"If you're not going to your dental appointment would you let me wear your mink stole?" My mother reached up and unhooked her mink stole and placed it around Mrs. Pearson's shoulders. I was not surprised because I had seen that generous spirit in my mother many times. *I remember the time when her younger sister, Mary, came to visit from Cincinnati, Ohio. Aunt Mary picked up my mother's wedding band from the living room* fireplace mantle. When she placed it on her finger the fit was perfect. She liked it so much she asked my mother.

"Sis, since you are not wearing this ring, would you give it to me?" Mother didn't like to wear jewelry so she gave her wide gold wedding band to her sister.

Mrs. Pearson left wearing Mother's stole to board the train, which ran from the head of Gary Hollow to Welch. On the way the train wrecked and threw Mrs. Pearson out of her seat. Somehow her head was caught. It broke her neck and she died instantly. Then our family realized God had used Otie's screams to protect our Mother from the train wreck. I was so sad that I didn't act like myself. I couldn't overcome the grief and neither could my mother. Mr. Pearson was so overcome with grief that shortly after his wife's death he moved away.

One day, while drinking a glass of milk, I was looking out the back door. Suddenly my eye caught something white on the step. I looked down. There sat Mrs. Pearson wearing her white nurses uniform, her white cap over her dark hair, and she looked so beautiful. When she smiled at me all the grief left me because I knew she was happy. I believe this was God's way of comforting me and my mother. However, Mother losing her best friend intensified her discontentment in Wilcoe. She was raised in a farm family where there was always fresh air, sunshine and fields between neighbors. This made her homesick for her parents and sisters, who still lived on farms in Virginia. Also, father working very long hours in the coal mines made Mother more fully responsible for the family and more lonely than usual. She worried about her husband coming home with coal dust on his body and wondered what his lungs looked like. Then, there were the smelly coke ovens across town from our house. There were two more passed the post office and company store, with railroad tracks between them. The igloo looking brick ovens with fireproof bricks burned a special kind of chuck coal. It burned to a certain stage before it was loaded on coal cars to be shipped to Pittsburg, Pennsylvania for the steel mills during World War I. Father decided Mother needed to move from the double house where Mr. and Mrs. Pearson had lived and had been such good friends. Since father didn't have any job training, other than farm work, he felt like he had to work in the mines so he moved the family to a rental house down the next block. My little neighbor friend, Ruth Dennison, persuaded my mother to let me go to school with her when I was five years old. That turned out to be a disaster. The very first day I caught lice from the girl that sat in front of me. When Mother found lice in my hair it shocked her. My father went to the drugstore for her. The pharmacist recommended 'Blue Pacific' and it killed my head lice. Because I would not turn six years old until August, mother decided to keep me home until the fall school year. I missed Ruth so much that I slipped off and went to school and sat under her window and softly called out to her. "Ruth, Ruth", when suddenly I realized I might get into trouble and I ran home.

When I was six years old the excitement of Christmas Eve had me hyper as Lena and I sat in the living room wondering what we would get for Christmas. Then I looked at the fireplace and asked my sister.

"As big as Santa is, how will he get down that chimney without getting dirty?"

Lena, being the quiet type, didn't get excited about things I would.

When Mother called us in for dinner, just as I got to the kitchen door, I saw Father putting a beautiful white cake with white icing and small red dots around the cake, up on top of the Sellers kitchen cabinet as I started to sit down to eat dinner. Later that evening Mother put me and my two sisters, Lena and Alma, to bed so she could finish all of her Christmas duties before going to bed.

As I lay there on my bed, trying to go to sleep, I couldn't forget about that cake Father had put on top of the cabinet and it got the best of me. Unknown to me, being only six, I didn't know that Father hadn't fastened the lighter top of the cabinet to the heavier cabinet bottom.

Finally, when I didn't hear any noise, I thought everyone was asleep. I eased myself out of bed as quiet as possible and walked to the kitchen door where I could see the cake still sitting up high on top of the cabinet. I thought. *I'll just drag a kitchen chair over here and then I can reach high enough to get just one little red dot off the icing.* I drug a kitchen chair from the table, placed it in front of the cabinet, climbed up and could not reach the top of the cabinet. Then the idea hit me to step up on the porcelain shelf, where my mother cut out the biscuits. I stepped up on the cabinet shelf and suddenly the whole top flew forward. It missed me! I found myself on the floor with the cake. The crash made a loud noise and Mother and Father came running down the steps and into the kitchen. After checking me over to see if I had been hurt, they both were so relieved that I was all right that they hugged me and took me back to bed. When I saw the looks on my parent's faces, I wished that I hadn't made the big mess on Christmas Eve. After that trick, I earned the reputation of 'bad child' from my family.

Christmas morning we ran down the steps to the living room. My parents never had a Christmas tree, when they were children, and we never had one either. Lena and I looked to see what Santa put in our stocking hanging under the mantle. Then we tore into the toys sitting on each side of the fireplace. Our parents decorated the living room with wreaths in the windows and greenery on the mantle. I got interested in toys and dinner and forgot to be upset over ruining our Christmas cake.

Shortly after that we moved near a church across the county road. The teacher, of the Primary Sunday school class, visited my mother and asked her if she could bring Lena and me to Sunday school. Mother gladly agreed and sent father to the company store for white material and she made matching dresses for my sister and I. Even though Lena was thirteen months younger than me, people thought we were twins. We both were about the same size. We were fair skinned with rosy cheeks and lips, big blue eyes and we both had snow white hair. While Father was at the store, he also bought four or five-inch-wide blue satin ribbon. Mother used the ribbon to tie around our waists and made a big bow in the back of our white dresses.

My father ordered a Beckwith Piano from Sears Roebuck and Company, accompanied by a cabinet for storing the rolls of music for the self-player. The piano was shipped to the Wilcoe train depot and from there it was hauled by horse and delivery wagon, called a dray, to our home.

A piano teacher, Miss Bowman, came to Wilcoe to spend the summer with relatives, who lived between Wilcoe and Welch. My mother hired her to give me piano lessons, even though I was only five years old and had not been to public school except that one day. I learned by memory to play a waltz called, 'Little Indian Boy'.

Our Sunday school teacher told us how God made a mud man and breathed the breath of life into him and he became a living soul. God named him Adam. As a five year old, I already had been making mud pies and creating saucers and cups out of the yellow clay I found at the edge of the back porch with strange red spots. I found a piece of a broken plate and scraped all the red spots off because I felt it wasn't clean. The next day I went out to play, and to my surprise all those red spots were back in the yellow clay as the day before. I called my father to solve the problem for me. He saw all the old red clay I had scraped off the day before and he knew I was telling the truth. After he left, not knowing what the spots were, *I thought what the Sunday school teacher taught us about God making a man.* I began to scrap all the red spots off the yellow clay again and made a man. There he laid! His body! His arms! His legs! His head! Suddenly it dawned on me! *"WHAT IF HE COMES ALIVE AND STANDS UP? WHAT WILL I DO?"* I became so scared! I took him, balled him up and threw him away. I ran into the house never to go back out there and play.

In the meantime my father told a miner he worked with what had happened with my clay and he asked the man.

"What do you think those red spots are?" The miner told him.

"Before you moved into that house a man was shot on that back porch. That could be his blood that ran down into the yellow clay."

My father worked long hours, in a mine, loading coal. One night he came home from working late. He looked in the dining room and there was the table set with a long white cloth. It looked like Mother had set the table as though we were having company. There was a man sitting at the foot of the table wearing a black suit, vest and white shirt and tie. On his vest was draped a long gold chain connected to his gold pocket watch. The man turned and looked at my father and when Father started to speak to him, the man vanished along with all the table setting.

One night after that, Father came in from working late again. Mother met him at the back door. She had on her usual long white night gown and her long dark hair was hanging around her shoulders. When father reached out to mother, she vanished. It scared Father. He ran upstairs and found her in bed sound asleep. After learning of the blood in the clay and these two strange experiences, my father finally decided to move his wife and family out of Wilcoe. After talking with a real estate agent, Mr. Hunt with Lilly Land Company of Princeton, West

Virginia, Father agreed that Mr. Hunt could take him and his family to Princeton looking at real estate. The next day, after looking at real estate, Father didn't feel that he wanted to move his family to Princeton. However, stranger than fiction, Father accepted a position with Lilly Land Company to sell real estate in the area of Kenova and Huntington while taking a home study course about 'How to Repair Mine Machinery and Electrical Equipment'.

In February, 1922, Mr. Hunt found us a large house to rent in Kenova. That house lasted a week. When the rains began, the Ohio River flooded and the water came into our house.

I began second grade in Kenova and a boy in my class gave me my first large beautiful valentine. Mr. Hunt moved us across town to higher ground into a four room house with a front porch across the front. The back porch had a room with a water toilet. The only bad thing about this move was I had to change schools. I walked up a steep hill and crossed six railroad tracks with the other children in our neighborhood. There was a watchman that let us know when we could or couldn't cross the tracks. The school wasn't as nice as where we had just moved from. If you can imagine an outhouse with four or five seats in a row over a metal trough, with a loud noise of water running under to a sewer pipe, that was our 'water toilet' at school.

At Easter time Mother colored eggs and put them in a basket of green grass for Lena and me to go across to the park for an Easter egg hunt. However, Easter morning when Lena awoke, she fell back in bed sick and had a high fever. The doctor came to the house and diagnosed my sister with Scarlet Fever and a 'Quarantined' sign went up on the post of the front porch. I was so disappointed and felt sorry for Lena. She was so sick and we couldn't go to the park. After the doctor pronounced that Lena was well, Mother had to wash all the bed clothes and hang them outside in the sun. The doctor brought a fumigator to disinfect the house. Mother fixed us a picnic lunch, closed all the doors and windows in the house, turned the fumigator on and we went to the park for the day.

Now that the quarantine had been lifted, Lena and I were going back to school on Monday. A few days later, just as it was with Lena, when I tried to get out of bed that morning, I fell back sick with fever and headache. Thereafter, my three month old brother, Otie, came down with Scarlet Fever along with me. Unbelievable, the 'Quarantined' sign was reposted on the front porch to our dismay. Not only did Otie have Scarlet Fever but Diphtheria and Spinal Meningitis. Therefore, to prevent us from developing Diphtheria, Doctor Garrett gave my two sisters and me, shots. To do this, he turned each one of us across his knees and shot us in our hips. The shot hurt so badly that it affected our ability to set down. Also, he painted our throats from ear to ear with iodine, which turned our skin real dark brown. After a while, the skin began to peel from our necks and we were brown and white spotted. I was glad we were Quarantined so our school friends wouldn't see us. My brother was so young, after a period of time he went into a coma and Doctor Garrett told my parents.

"Otie can't make it through the night and there is no more I can do for him." Father was determined to get help. He asked the doctor.

"Is there more modern help or someone to help us?" The doctor contacted Huntington Hospital and four doctors were sent to our house immediately. They covered my brother with a sheet of glass. The doctors agreed with Doctor Garrett. My brother would not live through the night and they left.

After the doctors left, our neighbor, Mrs. Gibson knocked on the door and asked if she could do anything for Mother. Mother told her the doctors gave her baby boy up to die. Mrs. Gibson replied.

"Do you believe in prayer?" Mother humbly told our neighbor.

"I'm a sinner and don't know how to pray."

"God can save you and heal your baby; there is nothing too hard for God."

Since World War I, crime had increased and Kenova had a ten o'clock curfew. Mrs. Gibson asked Mother.

"Would you allow members of my prayer group to slip in, after the curfew, to pray for your baby?" Mother reminded her that there was the 'Quarantine', also.

"We are not afraid."

Later that night, one by one, people began gathering in the living room with my baby brother. They prayed a fervent prayer of faith over him. Later, one of the women opened the kitchen door, where I was sitting with my parents, and excitedly, in a loud voice announced.

"I JUST GOT WITNESS FROM THE LORD THAT YOUR BABY IS HEALED. YOU GO IN THERE AND LOOK."

Mother jumped up and rushed into the living room and Baby Otie looked up at our Mother and smiled. He had come out of the coma. God replaced our mourning with gladness.

The next morning when Doctor Garrett arrived at our house, Otie was sitting on Mother's lap and we were all laughing and playing with him. The doctor asked.

"Where is the baby that was sick?" All of us, still laughing, pointed at the baby and told the doctor.

"That's him!" The doctor replied.

"This can't be the same baby."

Laughing, I told him. "That is the only baby we have."

During all the family sickness Father completed his home study course, and it paid off. My father got out of real estate and obtained a job at Gary number two as maintenance man repairing mining machinery and electrical equipment. To move the family back to Wilcoe, my father rented a double house adjoining the pastor of the Community church where, Lena and I had attended before.

My mother's attitude had changed about Wilcoe, not only because of what all the family had been through in Kenova, but the coke ovens were no longer burning. The steel mills of Pittsburgh, Pennsylvania, no longer needed the coke to make steel for the World War I equipment, since it ended in 1918.

Mother gave birth to her fifth child, Baby Edith Alice, soon after moving. This gave us another baby to love. My first day at school, my teacher, Miss Browning, the pastor's daughter, placed me back in second grade instead of letting me go on to the third grade. However, it wasn't long before I became friends with my classmates.

One day a boy named Hendrickson, across the aisle from me, wrote me a note. He flipped it across the aisle to me and it landed at my feet. I picked it up just as Miss Browning looked up. She said, "Vera, bring the note up here." Red-faced and terribly embarrassed, I finally got my legs to move and managed to carry myself up to her desk in front of the students. She took the note and sent me back to my seat. *To this day I don't know what the note said.*

After that, Miss Browning made me the 'teacher's pet'. Second grade was going to present the play, 'Little Bo Peep'. Since the school didn't have an auditorium, we were going to use the church platform. The teacher made up to me for embarrassing me in front of the class by picking me to be Little Bo Peep. Mother let my hair grow out for the role and Miss Browning came and took me to her home. She curled my hair with a curling iron in long ringlets and dressed me just like Little Bo Peep. I felt so pretty on stage. When my father saw how pretty I looked with curly hair, he went to Welch and purchased a curling iron. I learned to curl my hair.

The end of the second grade I was proud to be promoted to the third grade. We use to go out on the playground at recess and play, 'Sling Tag.' A long line of children, holding hands, marched in a circle and the last person was slung to the ground. Because I was the smallest one, I was always put on the end so I stopped playing. I would rather have played the calmer games such as 'Ring Around the Rosy' or 'Drop the Handkerchief'. We third grade girls liked to entertain ourselves by putting our coats on backwards, while someone would button the back. Then we would put our shoes on the wrong feet, laughing at each other.

I remember my fourth grade teacher, Miss. Sherry. I don't know why she got up from her desk and walked back and sat in the empty desk behind me. Vernon, across the aisle, watched the teacher squeeze her large body into that desk. When I looked back at Vernon, I knew he was trying to suppress laughing out loud from him shaking. My imagination was already causing me to shake with silent laughter. The teacher saw Vernon and me moving. When the teacher, unexpectedly, tapped me on the top of my head with a pencil, I immediately settled down. When school was out for the summer, my teacher went back to her hometown in Kentucky, and to my surprise, she wrote me a personal letter. All I remember about the letter is how she ended it. *"I have dahlias in my flower garden with blooms as large as dinner plates; almost as beautiful as your sweet face."*

In August, mother gave birth to her sixth child and the second boy, Edgar Paul; so we had another baby to love.

That summer before I went into fifth grade, our neighbor girl, Rena, asked my Mother.

"Could Vera go with me upon the hill to pick flowers?" We gathered armloads of Mountain Laurel and then she went on to her home. Instead of going straight down the street to my home, I decided to go between the coke ovens to visit with the hogs my father had in a pen. As I was walking I heard a voice, "Vera." I turned around and could not see one soul. I knew I was too far from home for it to be Mother, plus it was a strange voice. While I wondered whose voice I heard, I began walking towards home. Then I heard that same voice. *"The world needs you!" I realized it must be supernatural.* I became so happy! I didn't want to tell anyone because they might make fun of me. I continued to wonder what that meant. Shortly after that on a bright sunshiny morning, I walked out on the front porch. I saw people passing by our house from front and side streets, in the direction of the river. I asked someone what was going on. They told me. "A man saw a boy lying on the railroad tracks and he is dead." Then I learned that the Magistrate had arrived, ready to hold an inquest for the dead boy. I followed the crowd to hear that the boy had jumped from the moving train, expecting to hit on solid ground, and in the dark hit his head on a railroad tie as he landed. Later the newspaper reported that the boy went away from home to try to find a job during the summer months. Not having found a job he was returning home to his family, which lived up Saw Mill Hollow on a small farm.

I came home from school one afternoon. Mother had our baby brother, who was one year old, in her lap. His right leg was swollen and from his foot to the knee was twice the size. The doctor came to the house and reported that Edgar had blood poison in his leg. When Father came home from work, he immediately rushed him to Welch hospital. They wanted to amputate his leg to keep the poison from spreading throughout his body.

Father asked. "Can you think of any way you can save his leg?" The doctor said. "If you're willing to take a chance on his life, I will try." Father agreed. The surgeon made splits around his leg about an inch apart, covered the leg with black salve then wrapped his leg with a thick white bandage and sent him home for us to care for until he healed.

Right after that, Mother's weakness overcame her to the point that Father drove her to the Welch hospital for a checkup. The doctors reported that they could see a spot on her lungs and recommended that she be taken to a Tuberculosis hospital. Father hired a woman named Mamie, to keep us children and do housework. For six long weeks, Mother rested in the hospital until the doctor reported that her lungs were clear and sent her back home. They gave her instructions to eat a healthy diet, take walks and get plenty of fresh air.

One evening mother took my little sister and brother for a walk up to the schoolhouse. She could hear people singing a hymn in the school. She ran up the steps and into the school building. She sat the children beside her in the back of the room. After listening to the evangelistic sermon, Mother went to the altar. She accepted Jesus as her Savior. Before she left, the preacher prayed for her healing. God healed her from her weakness. The next evening when Lena and I entered the house from school, we heard someone singing in the kitchen. Also, we could smell good food cooking. I whispered to Lena. "Wonder if father rehired Mamie to work for us?" When we saw that Mother was out of bed, and in the kitchen singing and cooking, we were amazed. Thereafter, she ran her own home.

After school one afternoon, a group of us were walking down the sidewalk. Charles caught up with me and grabbed my body tightly in his arms and tried to kiss me. I struggled, determined that he was not going to kiss me, when his ear came in front of my mouth, I bit down. He let me go when I bit his ear.

He walked away like a real cool guy and avoided me after that incident.

That same summer Rena and I were walking to her house in the next block. For the first time, I noticed a culvert. When we got down and looked there was a light at the end of the culvert. We did not know the light was shining across streets and sidewalks and the railroad tracks were between the two coke ovens down in the town. We could not walk standing up. We bent over, which was very painful. Exhausted, we finally arrived at the end of the culvert. We thought we could walk out on the ground; instead it was the river and we had to turn around and walk almost an hour back through the culvert towards home. We agreed never to tell a soul how foolish we were. Water could have washed us into tug river and no one would have known where we were. *I awoke that night thinking what a dangerous thing we did.* I felt bad for days, afraid to tell anyone.

By the time I got to fifth grade there was a new girl in our class, named Angeline, who had just arrived from Italy. Her father had come to work as a stone mason in the area. She had beautiful coal black hair, which curled under around her face and turned under around the back of her neck. I loved her beautiful olive skin. One day Angeline was walking home with me and the other girls. Suddenly she stumbled over a rock and almost fell. I caught her and kept her from falling. She looked at me and said. "Oh, me like-a-fall." When a girl named Virginia heard her say that, she laughed and made fun of Angeline; I felt sorry for Angeline. I couldn't understand what caused Virginia to act like that, since her father had a good job on the railroad, and her family had a long black elegant car. Virginia, and her sister, wore store bought clothes of the latest fashion. The next day, the teacher had a spelling contest. She gave Virginia the word, 'pumpkin', to spell. She straightens herself up, so proud that she knew how to spell that big word. In a loud voice she said. 'punkin', p-u-n-k-i-n. The students and the teacher all began laughing. *The first thing I thought about was how she had made fun of Angeline. That day, I learned a lesson. It doesn't pay to make fun of other people.*

In the month of August, the temperature must have been one hundred degrees. Mother sent me across the street to the store. I ran into a schoolmate, Elsie, who lived at the end of Saw Mill Hollow. After greeting one another, she said.

"Aint it hot?" I agreed and told her.

"My bare feet are burning in the hot coal dust." She agreed.

"Mine too! We have the best swimming hole at my house." I told her.

"I would like to get into the water." She asked.

"Why don't you go home with me?" Excitedly I asked.

"How far is it?" Then she told me.

"It's just a little piece." I agreed to go swimming with her. About halfway up Saw Mill Hollow, I wanted to know.

"How much further is the place to swim?" She replied.

"Oh, it's just a little ways." I began worrying about being gone so long, but the thought of getting in cool water, under shade trees, got the best of my intentions. Unknown to me, Elsie lived at the very end of Saw Mill Hollow. Finally, when we arrived, I wanted to know.

"What are we going to wear swimming?" She told me.

"Just take your dress off and swim in your panties." The water wasn't deep. It came to our waist and we stooped down and let the water come over our shoulders. Just about the time I decided I'd better go to the store, and get home, I looked up and there stood my father. I jumped out of the swimming hole and put on my dress. When I didn't see my Father, I thought he had gone on ahead. When I arrived home, I knew Mother would be cooking dinner in the kitchen, so I sneaked in the front door. I tiptoed through the living room into the dining room, and hid beside our large buffet. I heard Father open the front door. I scooted down as far as I could get, hoping he would not find me. My father walked in the dining room and straight to the buffet and looked down at me. He was holding a long branch, which he had made into a switch. While holding the stick for me to see, he told me.

"Vera, do you see this?" Too scared to speak, I shook my head yes. He continued.

"If you ever slip off again, I'll use this switch on your legs. I was so relieved when I realized he wasn't going to switch me. I promised him that I would never slip off again. When I walked in the kitchen to face Mother, she made a promise.

"I will never send you to the store again." She didn't!

Father liked to play games with us children. We were playing dominoes at the dining room table. Suddenly, my mother said.

"Daddy, do you think it might be a sin to play dominoes? My father just laughed and kept on playing.

On Halloween night, we came in the house from the front porch. The dining room table was moving, and since we had been telling ghost stories on the front porch, that frightened us, until father crawled out from under the table cloth, laughing. His next project was to use the old coke ovens. Now that the coke ovens were no longer burning, Father decided to build a hog pen on the shelf in front of one of the entrances of the coke ovens. He bought two young pigs from a man, who owned a farm up Saw Mill Hollow. He fed them all summer and fall, until the first freeze. Father's first time hog killing at Wilcoe, was when I was eleven years old. I begged to go with him. He told me.

"You don't want to see that." I was so determined to go when I told him. "PLEASE, YES I DO!" Father laughed and told me.

"You can go." When we arrived at the hog slaughter, Father had already dug a hole in the ground and inserted a large steel barrel. He built a fire to heat the water. When I saw Father was going to shoot one of the hogs, I ran away from the hog pen and put my hands over my ears so I couldn't hear the shot. Then afterwards, I went to watch Father and his helper holding the hog's legs. He shoved it back and forth in the barrel of hot water. Next, as Father and his helper were scraping the hair off the hog, I also thought I could scrape the hog. When they gave me a scraper I tried to scrape the hair the best I could, but I couldn't do it as well as the men. I spent the rest of the day watching the men clean and hang the hog from the coke ovens.

Father brought a ham in the kitchen for our Thanksgiving and gave the pastor a ham. The pastor told Mother.

"Put an onion in the pot of water with the ham and boil the ham." That was the best holiday we had thus far.

At Christmastime, when Father killed the second hog, I didn't ask to go, since I already knew how they did it.

The Pastor and his family lived in the other side of our duplex. We had to speak softly because every word could be heard through the wall. That Christmas Mother asked my sister Lena to take the pastor's family a pound of home churned butter with a design on top and a quart of buttermilk. When Lena went next door and knocked on the pastor's door, he shouted.

"COME ON IN! "For the first time, Lena was startled as she viewed her first poker game in progress. She was shocked to see more money on the table then she had ever seen in her ten years. There the pastor, his wife, daughter and her young man and another engaged couple were all seated around the table holding a hand full of cards. The main reason this scene put fear in Lena's heart, she and I had found a deck of cards on the street a couple of weeks earlier; proudly we ran home shouting.

"MOTHER LOOK WHAT WE FOUND!" As we handed the deck of cards to Mother, she lifted the stove eye and as she put that deck of cards in the fire of our cook stove, she let us know these cards were the kind used to gamble; and it's a sin to gamble. Disappointed that we lost the cards as we turned to leave the kitchen, Mother told us.

"I don't want this kind of cards in my home."

A few days later a neighbor lady, who lived at the end of our block and across the street from the church we attended, knocked on our front door. When Mother opened the front door I heard the neighbor say.

"I need to talk to you. I don't know why my son stays until the wee hours of the night at the Pastor's house."

Mother invited our distraught neighbor into our dining room and they both sat down at the table. Mother motioned for everyone to be silent! As the two women sat at the table, periodically, the phrase, 'I bid', came through the wall in many different voices. However, finally, they heard the pastor raise his voice in anger to his wife.

"YOU TOOK ALL MY MONEY." Mother then invited the broken-hearted neighbor into the living room, where the next door neighbors wouldn't hear them talk. Mother shared with her how Lena was invited into the house and where six people were sitting around the table, cards in hand, and a lot of money on the table. They both came to the conclusion that the way this pastor lives reveals the kind of man that he is; usually a grandma called preacher and not called of God to preach the Gospel.

Chapter 2

While I was in sixth grade my friend, Ruth, started riding a bus in her seventh grade to Gary High School, about three miles away. Every Sunday morning Lena and I would go up the street and sit on Ruth's front porch until time for Sunday school. The first Sunday morning after Ruth had started seventh grade, her mother came out on the porch.

"Ruth is very sick and we had to take her to the Welch hospital." The day I saw Ruth's brother ride by the school on a work day, I knew something was wrong! When my sister and I arrived home from school, Mother told us that Ruth had died. *The first thing I thought of was the time, as a five year old, I sat outside of her school room window whispering, "Ruth, Ruth."* The funeral was beautiful with all the young girls carrying flowers and for weeks the community mourned the death of our friend Ruth.

That winter my mother was suffering with pains in the abdominal area. The doctor advised an operation. Father took her to Bluefield Sanatorium for an appendix and hysterectomy operation. My father stayed all day and night with her. When he came the next morning, they called him back and told him.

"Your wife has taken a turn for the worse." Immediately he left home and left us children with Mamie. I asked her.

"Do you think Mother will die?' *I thought Mother would die when I saw tears in her eyes. Suddenly, it came to my mind that God had healed my little brother, Otie.*

By the time I got upstairs to my room, I held my arms in the air and prayed.

"Lord, please don't let my mother die." After I said that I felt tears running in my ears. I felt peace and assurance that Mother would not die. I ran downstairs and told Mamie.

"Mother is not going to die." Several days later, Father brought Mother home from the hospital. It wasn't too long before she took charge of her house again.

In Wilcoe, below our home, there was a railroad side track where they parked the little red caboose. The doctor told my father.

"A man is in that caboose and he has Small Pox and I fear an epidemic will hit our town. I advise every person to be vaccinated." Father took Lena and me to the clinic at Gary Number 2 to be vaccinated.

After a couple of days, where I had been vaccinated looked infected. Father took me back to the doctor. I had to wear a bandage above where I had been inoculated and the doctor put my arm in a sling, which relieved some of the pain.

Mrs. Martin, my Sunday school teacher, let her nine year old daughter, Juanita, come to our home and play with me and my younger brothers and sisters. A June bug landed on the banister of the porch and I grabbed it. I held the bug, while Lena went in the house to get the ball of twine. As Juanita watched, Lena held the June bug while I tied the string to one of its legs and the three of us girls watched the June bug fly a couple of times around in a circle. Suddenly I became afraid its leg would come off and I untied the string and turned it loose.

In mid-life Mrs. Martin had a baby girl and her nine year old daughter, Juanita, named the baby Precious. Juanita loved her new baby sister so much that Mrs. Martin let the baby sleep with her. When Precious was a toddler, one night she rolled over on Juanita's arm and the baby's eye came in contact with Juanita's vaccination for Small Pox. The doctor said.

"The serum from Juanita's arm has taken in the baby's eye and she could lose her eye." He put a patch on the baby's eye and one on Juanita's arm so that couldn't happen again.

Later when Precious regained her sight in that eye, the doctor put glasses on her to strengthen the eye. *Years later, when I had my second daughter, I named her Juanita.*

The summer before I was going into seventh grade, Mother gained strength and wanted to work and make money. The railroad started building a tunnel and someone told Mother.

"The men don't like the food at the YMCA. Mother saw, besides doing her housework, where she could make a little money. She sent word to the construction men.

"You can come to my home and eat three meals a day, if you choose." About eight men happily sent word back to her that they would be there for meals. So Mother hired Sally to help her around the house. My mother served buckwheat pancakes or gravy and eggs, and the best homemade biscuits for breakfast. For lunch and dinner, Mother always served a full meal. She would have beans and greens with cornbread or country fried steak with potatoes, macaroni and cheese or potato salad. She served coffee, homemade pies and cakes for dessert.

One man paid her his monthly fee, for three meals a day, and Mother didn't remember where she put the money. She searched the house and finally gave up looking for the money. When wintertime came, and there was no work to be done in the garden, my father picked up the family Bible from the library table in the living room. He put that big Bible on his lap. When he opened it, there was Mother's money.

Before Mother began having boarders, a man came to the front door and told Mother.

"I am hungry and need some food." Instead, she gave him money to go to the company store to buy something to eat. The preacher, next door, heard Mother giving the stranger money for food. He told my mother. "I never give money to any tramps that come to my door." My mother replied.

"How do you withhold feeding or giving the money to the hungry without telling a lie?" Our pastor shared his secret of not telling a lie to Mother.

"I have a pocket, which is named, 'the World' and it never has anything in it. Therefore, when I tell a beggar I don't have a cent in the 'World' I am not lying." The pastor turned and went back in his duplex.

Once the rumors got around town that our pastor helped himself to fruits and vegetables from the grocery store, held poker parties at the parsonage, and lied about not having money, the officials forced him to resign.

While the preacher was standing on the porch of the store, the man came out of the store and sat down on the porch's top step, opened the brown bag and ate his lunch. (My mother was right!)

After the pastor moved out of the duplex, Pastor Martin, his wife and pre-school age son David, became our new neighbors.

As our old pastor used to come out on the porch every morning whistling, Pastor Martin came out on the front porch every morning wearing his clerical collar and watched the people going to and fro around the town. The pastor's wife was a recluse and seldom left the house and took care of their pre-school son.

As a sixteen year old teenager, I thought this pastor's sermons were dry and boring. However, a few weeks later when our church held a revival, Evangelist Johnson livened up the town. Lena and I went to the revival every night with our Father, who thought that Evangelist Johnson was an excellent old fashioned, fire and brimstone preacher.

After the first night of service, Father told me on the way home.

"He makes Heaven seem so real."

The next night, during the Evangelist's sermon, suddenly we heard large hail stones hitting on the church's tin roof. Everyone was scared and some began weeping. Even with Father being beside me, I began crying from fear. The Evangelist said.

"Let's all get on our knees and pray." Father, Lena and I followed the people running to the altar. All of us young people were crying because we were scared. About ten minutes later we didn't hear the hail and the whole congregation jumped up from the altar and ran outside to see what had happened. We were shocked to see flat dirty hail piled up all over town. The piles were six inches deep and were about one inch in diameter and shaped like a flat wafer.

The worst part was when we put our feet down to walk on top of the hail it slid under our feet. Everyone had to put their feet under the pile of ice and slide their feet along the street. Father tried to answer my question.

"Why is the hail dirty, I asked?" He said.

"Maybe it cleaned the coal dust out of the air as it came down." The air did smell cleaner.

Needless to say the next night the town, old and young people, showed up at church with an overflow of people standing outside. All ages crowded around the altar after the Evangelist's sermon.

A couple days later, Mother invited Pastor Martin's family next door and the Evangelist to our home for lunch. The Pastor refused to eat with Evangelist Johnson because he preached hell fire and brimstone.

However, at lunch Father was seated at the head of the table and our family was seated around the table with the Evangelist. Near the end of lunch, Father asked the Evangelist.

"I don't feel right. What must I do to be saved?" I sat there wondering what the Evangelist was going to say to my father because I wanted to know also. He replied.

"The only thing I know to tell you to do is pray until the bell rings clear."

After the two week revival, most of the town attended after the hail storm. The Evangelist left town and Pastor Martin had the honor of holding a baptismal service for the ones that made a profession of faith believing in Jesus Christ. I joined the church and almost all the other young people in the church plus the many adults who were in the service.

A week or two after the town returned to normal living, Lena and I came home from school to find Mother upstairs in bed crying. When I went closer, I saw Mother was shaking from head to toe and looked as if she was in shock. I said.

"Mother, what's wrong?" Between broken words and sobbing she explained.

"Pastor Martin knocked on the front door. I invited him to step into the living room. Once in the house, he proceeded to put his hands on his hips and began rebuking me.

"What do you mean joining that old holy roller church? You know no one goes to that church but trash." The Pastor's condemnation of her in her own home while her husband was at work caused her a temporary nervous breakdown. The doctor said.

"That preacher should be horse whipped." Soon thereafter, Pastor Yates replaced Pastor Martin in the duplex next door.

Pastor Yates earned the reputation of a gentle man with a calling of God to preach the Gospel. Mother and his wife became the very best of neighbors. Lena and I enjoyed his daughter Mary, a senior just one year ahead of me.

Mary felt better starting to Gary High School, since Lena and I would be starting with her. Within the week a high school senior boy, Matt, saw Mary standing in the hall for the first time and fell 'head over heels' in love with her.

Matt and his family lived across town and his Father ran the local general store. The next Sunday Matt told his parents.

"I will be going to church where Mary's Father is the pastor." His parent replied.

"You can't leave our denomination!"

Matt's family became angry that their son came to our church but he made the long foot journey to our church every Sunday just to sit in church with Mary anyway. I would watch them. There was no secret in the way they looked at each other that they were in love.

One day Mary's Mother and my mother were standing on the front porch, when a man came across the street. Mrs. Yates asked Mother.

"Who is that man?" Mother told her.

"That's Matt's Father." Mrs. Yates said.

"He looks like a foreigner." Mother replied.

"He's of German decent."

This news added fuel to the fire that Matt had given up the family religion to date Mary and she told my mother.

"Just wait until I tell her Father. We don't want our son married to a foreigner. We aren't happy that Mary isn't dating someone in our denomination."

Towards the end of their senior year in desperation, Mrs. Yates made a bargain with Mary. "If you will break-up with Matt and promise me you will never marry him, I will buy you a new outfit."

Now in those years we had very few clothes, that was why the closets are so small in older homes. Usually, one or two good outfits for church, funerals or weddings and three or four outfits for school. Therefore, Mary agreed to the proposition her mother made with her.

Two weeks after graduation, Mary wore her brand new outfit when she eloped with Matt.

They did live together until 'death do us part' to her parent's disappointment.

Our pastor's two daughters invited Lena and me to go to a tent meeting Saturday night. We were standing on the outside of the tent listening to music, when a tall good looking man from Welch walked up to us. The Pastor's family knew this young man from their former ministry and they introduced me to Will Ed. The next Sunday evening, he got off the bus in front of my house and wanted to spend the evening with me. I told him. "I go to church on Sunday evenings." He walked to church with Lena, me and our friends. Will Ed stopped at the back row and sat down; the rest of us went on to the choir loft for our service. Afterwards, Will Ed walked me back home to wait for the next bus. I knew, since my friends and I were church going youth, I would never see him again once he waved at me as he boarded the bus. Unbelievable, the next Saturday he got off the bus and I invited him in the house to meet my parents and siblings and my mother liked him.

Later she advised me.

"Will Ed would make a good match for you." He had a winning personality and talked about interesting subjects.

Another day he arrived with a friend who had a car. His friend began dating my sister Lena.

One Sunday afternoon we drove to Welch to a movie and afterwards, Will Ed invited Lena and me to come to his home for Christmas dinner to meet his family. Somehow he got the impression that I would marry him and he didn't know that I was writing love letters to a guy named Curt, who had moved out of the area. Christmas at Will Ed's home looked like winter wonderland and a very elegant dinner was served. I liked Will Ed's parents and they seemed to enjoy having Lena and me for the special occasion. However, later Curt heard of me dating Will Ed and stopped writing to me. Not very long after Christmas, Will Ed lost his job and he moved to Horsepen, Virginia, with his parents.

Our Sunday school teacher planned a church picnic upon Peel Chestnut Mountain. The morning of the picnic, I got up early to make meringue for the two dozen butterscotch tarts. I packed them safely in a flat box, because we were going on a hay ride up the mountain. However, when my mother saw how many young people were on the truck, she turned around, looked at Lena and me, and shouted. "You can't go." I was so embarrassed to go out and tell the driver, "We won't be going."

The beginning of my seventh grade was my first experience of riding a school bus. I began riding the bus to Gary High School. It took a while for me to get use to changing classes, having different teachers and the crowds in the hallway. My English teacher told us there was a 'Declamation Contest' with speakers representing each grade. She chose me to represent the English class. When I finished reciting the poem, the seventh grade through the senior classes stood to their feet; boys whistled and the girls cheered me. However, sadly, the school superintendent's daughter won the contest, instead of me. Nevertheless, when I began Home Economics, I was the star of making biscuits. My teacher, Mrs. Daugherty, was surprised at my age that I could make such perfect biscuits. Mother let me make biscuits at age $9\frac{1}{2}$ because I begged her.

Lawrence's mother gave a fellowship party for the young people at church. She took me out to her flower garden to look at her flowers. The climbing red rose caught my attention. She asked me if I would like to plant one of those? I asked her.

"How will I plant it?" She told me to stick the stem in the ground and cover it with a quart Mason jar. After she cut one off, I took it home and planted it as instructed. Years later, when we visited Wilcoe, how excited it made me to see that someone had built a trellis beside the front porch and my red roses covered it and shaded the front porch.

⁓⃝

For my sixteenth birthday, Mother asked a friend, Inez and my sister Lena, to give me a surprise party. My friend, from down on the railroad yard, Bea, came to our home and told me they were going to play croquet that afternoon. Also, my boyfriend, Curtis and his brother 'Fats', who lived near Bea, kept me away from my house for the rest of the day. Afterwards, we sat on the back porch, while Bea's mother served us refreshments.

Later that evening, my friends walked home with me and I still didn't suspect anything. However, when we entered the front door, a large group of my friends shouted. "Happy Birthday!"

Each one threw a handful of peanuts in the shell at me. After we played many games, my mother and sister served birthday cake, fudge, party sandwiches and punch before I opened my beautiful gifts. They gave me pajamas, a compact, box of chocolates, box of stationary and a photo album, which I still have at 99 years young. Then a couple of months later, Mother let me have a Halloween party at our home. Lena and I told all our friends in high school and church. "Come to our party and bring all your friends and have everyone bring a white sheet."

They did! There were over one hundred young people that came. They came from Wilcoe, Welch, Havaco and all up and down Gary Hollow. After a treat of hot cocoa and cake, we put our white sheets over our heads. We marched silently, two by two, around town celebrating Halloween as ghosts. Later, everyone left for home and the next day at school the students were still talking about the party.

When I was in the eighth grade, I debated a classmate. To win the debate, we both held notes of points we wanted to make. Mine was in the affirmative. I had over prepared and didn't need my notes and won the debate, hands down. While I was still at Gary High School, a girl from another class came up to me and introduced herself.

"My name is Esther Hill." *I didn't know at the time, but learned much later, that she belonged to the church where my mother attended.* Esther made a point to get acquainted with me and we became good friends for the rest of our school time.

In the meantime, the assistant manager of the Company Store went to Pulaski, Virginia, and brought back a bride, Mary. Mary began attending church with Lena and me and suggested forming a quartet, since she was a good alto. Being a few years older than me, and married, didn't keep us from becoming good friends. Once we added a tenor, bass and soprano we had a great quartet that became popular in the area. I played the piano for us. We traveled around the area, riding in Edward's light tan model A Ford, singing at different churches. I felt sad for Father when I learned that the mines shut down and he would be working only two nights a week.

While still in high school, a new beautiful brick elementary school had been built in Wilcoe. A teacher, Miss Bowman, also attended our church. When she met our large group of young people she decided to put on the play, 'The Wild Oats Boy.' She gave me the staring role as the girlfriend of the Wild Oats Boy. *He wanted to marry me, but he wasn't a Christian. While I was attending church, he would be going dancing and sewing his wild oats. We quarreled and broke up. He finally, after a long time, became a Christian.* When we were planning the play, there had to be an intermission. Miss Bowman suggested that we get a singer. I told the teacher.

"A student from Gary High School, Esther Hill, has a good voice and she has sung in high school plays." When I mentioned Esther's name Virginia butted in and said.

"Oh, we don't want her." She hurt my feelings. *I remembered how she had hurt the new girl, Angeline, who had just arrived to our grade school from Italy.* Miss Bowman interrupted. "Ask Esther to come to the next rehearsal." When the teacher heard Esther sing, she put her on the program after she finished singing. She sung 'When The Moon Comes Over the Mountain'. The audience gave her a standing ovation. I felt happy that I won another victory over Virginia.

The day I learned that Esther went to church with my mother, she and her brother, Ernest, came to Sunday dinner. The whole family gathered around the table for a chicken dinner and fellowship. Afterwards the young people, along with the church quartet, arrived while they were singing. Suddenly, a floor lamp, beside the piano where I sat, shot fire up to the ceiling and startled me to the point I didn't want to play the piano that afternoon. Esther came over and put her arm around my shoulder to comfort me. I calmed down, after Father discovered the coating had worn off the lamp cord causing it to short and catch fire. It was fastened to a socket in the ceiling.

At high school, the end of the following week, someone told me.

"Esther had an appendix attack and is in the Welch hospital. The following Sunday, my longtime friend, Lawrence told me.

"Esther has died." I began crying because I would never see my good friend again. Later, Lawrence told me.

"Esther said, she would like to see you." I began crying again and wished that I could have gone to visit her. Then I met the new company store clerk, Willard Duncan, who lived across the street over the company store. He began writing me love notes and sent them to me when Lena went grocery shopping. We began dating regularly until my father surprised me with a move out of the area to Glenwood Park in West Virginia.

When I almost ended the eleventh year at Gary High School, the 1930 Depression disrupted many families and Father had to look for other means to support us. One Sunday afternoon our living room was full of young people, and the quartet was practicing. Someone knocked on the door. When I opened the door, there stood a strange man.

"My name is Mr. Owens. Is Mr. Lineberry home?" I told him.

"Father should be home soon. Would you like to come in and wait for him?" Mr. Owens gave me this shocking news.

"In the morning, "I'm moving your family to Glenwood Park." I had never heard of that place.

"Where is Glenwood Park?" Mable Grubb, a friend from church, spoke up and told me.

"It's over next to Bluefield, West Virginia." Mr. Owens left to go spend the night with his sister in Welch. He wanted to get an early start the next morning. After church that night, Lena and I were so upset. We told our parents about Mr. Owens stopping by our house.

"Why didn't you tell us we were going to move?" We ran upstairs to have a good cry.

April 1930, Mr. Owens got all the essentials we'd need to spend the night in Glenwood. Once we arrived at our new home, which rented for eight dollars a month, we were so disappointed. There were no utilities in the house, such as no water, no electricity, and no wall boards on the two by fours in the kitchen. Of course, being the oldest child, it was my duty to go out back to pump the water into the bucket and carry it up the steps to the kitchen for all the cooking, laundry and baths. Lena and I couldn't get the business courses at the High School and to my sorrow we felt like we had to quit school.

We moved to the Thornton home, where we had running water and a more modern house. My sister, Lena, was steadily dating Bernard. He would come to the house every Saturday night and bring his cousin Harry to visit with me. They would arrive late in the evening because they lived on connecting farms. Therefore, both of the men had to milk the cows, feed chickens and feed the horses and cattle before they arrived. Bernard and Lena sat on the couch and talked with each other. Harry and I sat in separate chairs on the other side of the room and he was a good conversationalist with a good sense of humor. When he would tell something funny, my sister and her date would join in with us.

After a short period of time, Harry turned his farm over to his brothers and joined the Citizen's Conservation Corp Camp (CCC Camp), established during the Great Depression of the 1930's to put people back to work. Later when he began writing friendly letters, I answered him.

However, unknown to me, Harry had come back home for a visit with his family from CCC Camp. During those years, few families had telephones and there wasn't the communication we are used to today. Anyway, Saturday night I invited Harold to come to my house because I was giving a party for some of my friends. There Harold and I sat together, when Harry walked in the house with Bernard. I will never forget the disappointed look on his face when he saw me with another young man. That was the last time I saw Harry.

Father drove us to the shirt factory in Princeton, for our first job. After we were hired, we walked from our house less than a mile, to catch the streetcar for five cents each way, to get to work and back. A few weeks after Lena and I were settled in our new job, Father got a job working in the mines at Winona. He rented a nicer home closer to Princeton. There Lena and I met Jim the janitor, who had traded his wife and many children for Sue, his mistress. Sue, who worked on the same operation with Mary and me, should have had the same number of bundles at the end of the day. However, after Mary and I finished our first bundle and went back for another one, they were all gone. Jim would bring Sue a new bundle every time she finished one. She never ran out of work and she didn't have to walk to the other end of the factory to get a new one. In order to keep down trouble, Mary and I asked to be put on another operation where we wouldn't run out of work. Our boss, Mr. Golden, placed me on a new operation and another double needle machine. As soon as I got settled, I happened to look up to see who my neighbors were. I saw a young man sitting almost directly in front of me, with a mile wide smile. I recognized him as the same young man who had picked up my pencil on his way to talk to his girlfriend. *As I sat thinking, what a beautiful blond girlfriend he had,* my work mate said to me. "He went over there to break up with her because she smokes."

The next morning, when I arrived at the factory, the young man met me at the door and handed me a note with that same mile wide smile. I smiled back, took the note and went to my sewing machine and put the note in my pocketbook and began to work. *As I worked that day I thought about my boyfriend, Byron, nicknamed Shorty, in Austinville, Virginia.* He came to my home every Sunday with his friend, Pete, who came to visit Lena. I assumed someday, I would marry Shorty because he was so good to me. Every time he came he brought me a box of candy and went to church with us. Shorty had a beautiful car. If I married him, we would live in a beautiful company home in Austinville, where I met him when Lena and I spent the winter with Aunt Flora's daughter, Hazel. That evening, getting ready for company, I opened my pocketbook to get my lipstick out, and there I saw that note. It said, "Dear Vera, You are the most beautiful girl I've ever met and I would like to date you, Love Harold." *Immediately I thought, I am in trouble because I am steadily dating Shorty.*

The next morning, the young man named Harold met me at the door, again. We began walking over to get our first bundles for the day. I told him.

"I am going steady with a man from Austinville."

"Did you read my note?"

"I'm sorry but I am going steady." When I walked away from Harold I felt badly because he had a disappointed look on his face. However, he continued to smile at me every time I looked up; I became embarrassed and wouldn't look in his direction anymore.

The next morning when I went to get my first bundle for the day, Harold handed me another note. Again, that night in my room, I read.

"I would like to date you if you're not engaged to Shorty. Please let me know. Love, Harold." *I thought about how to soften my answer to him.* The next morning I said.

"I'm older than you and I have a younger sister I would love for you to meet." He smiled at me.

"I accept your invitation to come to meet your sister at seven-thirty on Saturday night."

Lena and I had purchased some white organdy fabric with black polka dots. Since Lena had made her dress the Saturday before, I made mine the Saturday that Harold was coming to visit Edith.

After supper, I tried my dress on and before I had time to take it off, a knock sounded at the door. Not thinking it might be Harold, I opened the door and there he stood. He was smiling at me and commented.

"Oh, you look beautiful in your dress." I invited him to sit on the couch in the living room, while I went to get my sister. She had disappeared from the house! I went back and sit on the other end of the couch.

"I could not find my sister." He smiled and moved next to me and placed his arm around my shoulders and drew me closer to him.

"You are the one I want." Immediately I felt a thrill, which I had never felt before. I knew this is the man I will marry. He saw the look on my face and asked.

"How old do you think I am?" When he told me he was born February 8, 1917, I figured he was only two and a half years younger than me. He gave me time to think about it and then he said.

"Age doesn't matter if you love each other." I thought of my cousin, Hazel, who married a man twenty years older than she and how happy they were. I knew Harold was right. Hazel use to laugh and say.

"Well, you know they say, 'It's better to be an old man's darling rather than a young man's slave.'" *Thinking about Hazel, I looked at the man with his arm around me.*

"I suppose you're right." At that moment, my mother came running into the living room barefooted and walked straight to her bedroom. She didn't even see Harold. Harold got up and opened the door. He walked back to his home on Oakvale Road, on the other side of Princeton.

The next day, Harold was standing in front of the bundles. When I went to get my work, he handed me another love note. I put it in my pocketbook until I got home. It read: *"I love you very much and I'm looking forward to seeing you again". Love, Harold."* Three or four more days of love notes, I was standing beside Harold to get my first bundle for the day. Before picking up his bundle, he leaned over in a low voice and asked.

"Will you marry me?" I laughed and replied.

"Oh, you're kidding me." He said.

"No I'm not; I am serious and I want you to think about it." We both got our bundles and walked to our machines. I began thinking seriously about marrying Harold and all the problems we'd have without him having a good job. That day Harold told me.

"I have already applied for a job on the new road, between Bluefield and Princeton. I will know by tomorrow if I get the job." I laughed and half teasing, I told him.

"I will marry you if you get that job." I just knew he wouldn't get it! The next morning Harold arrived at work with that mile wide smile and told me.

"I got the job! I will start to work when the men begin building the forms for the cement. Gleason and I will be greasing the forms ahead of the cement truck." *Suddenly, I remembered to write Shorty a letter to tell him that I had become engaged to Harold Reed.*

The next week my husband-to-be began his new job greasing the forms on the construction site. Since the rains continued the next day, I worked on making my wedding dress. I used blue flat crepe fabric. The dress had a white satin ruffle in front of the neck with a row of gardenias at the base of the ruffle. The ruffle continued around the neck and met in the center to form a narrow collar, which hung over a blue short cape lined in white satin. The elbow length sleeves had an insert of white satin in a sleeve pleat. After working for about two weeks, one night during a hard rain Harold asked his brother-in-law, Walter, to drive him over to my house. That evening, when Harold arrived, he told me.

"If the rains continue enough to make the road muddy, so we can't work, tomorrow will be our wedding day. Harold and I decided to elope and not tell anyone until he got his first paycheck. I told my fiancé.

"Meet me at the streetcar station in the morning, where I will be in the restroom changing into my wedding clothes."

The next morning, I packed my wedding dress, white shoes, white gloves and white hat in a brown paper bag to cut down on suspicion. Lena and I boarded the streetcar heading towards Princeton. I told my sister.

"I have to get off at the next station. I already told her I was going to be a witness for my friend, Lucille, at her wedding. Once I changed into my wedding outfit, I came out of the restroom and saw Harold waiting for me. We rushed out and got into the backseat of Walter's car and his wife greeted us.

That morning, my friend, Lucille had been dropped outside the shirt factory instead of going to work. She walked down the street to meet us. She was going to witness my wedding instead of me witnessing hers. *The one thing that concerned me was, if it would stop raining before we got married. I'd always heard it would be bad luck to be married on a rainy day.* Lucille sat in the backseat with Harold and me and he kept his arm around my shoulder and held my hand all the way to Pearisburg, Virginia. Walter and his wife, Georgia, and Lucille went into the courthouse where we got our marriage license. At the courthouse a person told us of a minister, who lived on the corner across the street. The five of us walked across the street. The rain had stopped and the sun was shining bright by the time we knocked on the minister's door. The minister opened the door, all dressed, and seemed in a hurry to go to an appointment. However, he took the time to say a fast ceremony over us, which we could barely understand because he talked so fast. All we cared to hear him pronounce was, 'you are man and wife'. Harold kissed me, as his new bride, before paying the minister ten dollars. When I got home my oldest brother came in and his face was white as a sheet.

"Vera, I heard something I don't believe." I looked at him.

"What did you hear?" He said.

"I heard you got married." I replied.

"Oh, Otie you can just hear anything." When I went into the streetcar station the maintenance man, who was our neighbor, saw me coming out of the restroom dressed up and leaving with Harold.

A few days after getting married, Harold and I were standing outside with our arms around each other. Mother opened the door and saw us. I told my husband.

"You go on home and let me face Mother by myself." I went into the house and got my marriage certificate.

"See Mother, we are married." Mother looked to see if Harold was still outside. When she saw him, she called him to come into the house. She told us.

"You and Harold spend the night here." This was our first wedding night.

One week later, Harold and I were sitting outside under a large crab apple tree on a metal glider, when we heard loud noises. About fifteen or twenty people showed up in front of Harold and me beating on pots, pans, and ringing cow bells and other utensils. Suddenly, two men grabbed hold of Harold and me and drug us down the road and set us on a wagon seat, and a neighbor man drove us out to Glenwood Park and back home where we all celebrated together.

Harold and I wanted to rent an apartment in a big white house across from the shirt factory on Mercer Street. When we went to the house to look at the upstairs apartment, we liked it and we could afford the rent. We hadn't been able to afford a wedding ring and the landlady kept looking at my ring finger. Finally, she said.

"Someone else asked for this apartment before you." *Why hadn't she taken the rent sign down?*

We left there and rented a house on Straley Avenue. It was a vacant room, about 20 x 20 for five dollars a month. We had to share the bathroom down the hall with two other renters. Also, Harold and I purchased a miniature cook stove, which burned either wood or coal. Our landlady allowed the coal truck, from City Coal Company, to dump a ton of coal in her basement. My husband had to go downstairs, out the front door, around the back and on the side of the house to the door that led into the basement. He had to fill a bucket and carry it back upstairs for our cooking and heating. Harold's Mother gave us a metal bed frame with metal springs. It looked so old and worn that I was ashamed of it.

Saturday morning I went to G. C. Murphy and purchased a bright pink sateen fabric and white cording. I used one of my mother's old blankets to pad the headboard of the bed. I pulled the pink slip cover with white cording over it. I cut button shape circles out of cardboard, padded them with cotton and covered those buttons with white material. I used seven buttons on the slip covers, which gave it a professional look. When Harold's Mother saw that old bed, she had just given us, she shook her head.

"Is that the same bed I just gave you?"

Later I purchased flowered curtains for two windows in the apartment. For a closet, I purchased an extra pair of curtains to hang on a rod, which hung behind the entrance door to the apartment. Harold's brother-in-law, Walter, gave us a table about 30 x 45 inches wide and two chairs to use. I went to Murphy's for a white cloth to put on the table. We purchased a tall narrow cabinet, from McNutt Furniture store, for storage. Harold and I were very proud of our first cozy home together. When we were first married the winter of '35 and '36 was cold and snowy from October to March. We didn't see much of the ground because it was white so much.

One morning we were in a hurry to get to work, and as I looked down at the steps I saw, to my dismay, bedroom slippers on my feet! *I thought the hurrieder I get, the behinder I get!*

The shirt factory was ice cold until almost noon. This wasn't good for my health. I suffered with aching legs and sore throat most every morning. The doctor said my tonsils had to come out because they were dripping poison on my left bronchial tube causing a sore spot there.

During the surgery, as I was taking ether to put me to sleep, I kicked the nurse under the chin trying to get the lid off of my coffin. The nurse laughed about it later. The doctor gave me Aspergum to chew to ease the pain. He also gave me Cod Liver Oil to build up my strength. Harold spent the night in the doctor's office, on Mercer Street, in case I might start bleeding. Mr. Wright took us home in his car. We stayed on Reed Hill with Harold's family until I was able to walk home on Knob Street. We had an apartment in Hogan's home. We had 3 rooms, bath and a balcony. We enjoyed living there.

The Royal Theater was a short walk from our home. We went each Friday night to a serial called 'Phantom City', with Gene Autry, that we enjoyed very much.

We went for a walk on Harrison Street one evening. A man driving a truck stopped and told us that Nathan, Harold's brother, was in a saw mill explosion and was in the hospital. We hurried up there to see about him. Nathan had gained consciousness and was able to talk to us. His eye was swollen shut and some of his teeth had been knocked out. He was suffering from shock and had a lot of bruises, but he was alive.

The next evening, while visiting Nathan, I asked what he would like to have to eat. He said, "Fried oysters!" We stopped at the A & P Store on Mercer Street and bought a pint of oysters. We took Nathan a plate full and he ate all of them before we left. He said.

"Thank you Vera. That really hit the spot."

Later on Nathan got a job with Walter, who was working on a tunnel, to carry water underground into the city of New York in case they were bombed during the war they would still have water. When he found a house his mother and sister, Naomi, went to Shenarock to live with him.

In our upstairs apartment we began our first Christmas by setting up a little live tree. Harold went out on the hill where his family lived and cut down a four foot cedar tree for me to decorate. I went to Murphy's and purchased silver tinsel and small red and green colored balls for the tree.

Christmas Day my father showed up in his 1927 gray Dodge, four door sedan, and drove us to spend Christmas Day with my family. The heavy snow covered the ground in the zero weather. My sister Lena still lived at home and became engaged to Clifford. Until I got married Lena and I were so close not only in age but in spirit. The family held off dinner waiting for Clifford. An hour had passed and, when he hadn't arrived, Mother served dinner. After dinner, my sister took me in her bedroom to show me the white dress shirt lying on a shelf in the wardrobe, which she had bought for Clifford for Christmas. When we walked up to the wardrobe, the door was standing wide open and she said.

"Vera, every time I come into my bedroom that door is standing wide open and I have to close it. It has never done that before. Since the bedroom is off the living room I would see if anyone came in my room."

In those days the majority of homes did not have telephones, therefore, Lena had no way of contacting his family. We worried because he had always been punctual and especially on Christmas Day, when he and Lena were looking forward to exchanging gifts. As my father drove Harold and me home late that evening, Lena still hadn't heard from Clifford. I couldn't help but think about the strange door and went to sleep worrying about Clifford.

The next morning Harold and I, Lena, Clifford's mother and sister arrived without Clifford at the shirt factory. Mrs. Warren asked.

"Has anyone seen my son?" She had been out most of the night contacting Clifford's friends inquiring about her missing son. Someone spoke and said.

"Clifford went hunting with us yesterday morning and we got lost from him. When we didn't see him again, we decided he went home because of the cold weather." When Harold and I began working, Mrs. Warren and her daughter left the factory.

A couple of hours later the word spread.

"They found Clifford and he was sitting by the railroad track frozen stiff." Being one of our fellow workers, we all were too shocked to work. Harold and I took my sister Lena to the streetcar station and went to my parent's home to mourn the death of Clifford.

We lived in the upstairs of the two-story home until the weather began to get warm and we began planning to move before the hot summer. After being married over a year, the construction on the Bluefield Road had come to an end. Harold was hired by the State Road, in Mercer County, for the winter months to shovel cinders onto the slick roads. First of spring, Harold went back to work at the shirt factory. I'd had my tonsils taken out and I was still too weak, and my husband forbid me to go back to the factory to work.

In May my father informed Harold that they were hiring painters in Wilcoe. He had to go to Gary to apply with Mr. Thompson for a job. He refused to hire him. When he told my mother that he hadn't gotten the job, she told him.

"You go right back down there and keep going until you get a job." It took two more times until he got hired as a painter. In the meantime, Harold took the letter from the Virginian Railroad office, in reference to his father's death, and applied for the apprenticeship as the oldest son. At seven years old Harold's father, George, an engineer on the railroad, did not know there had been a rock slide on the track. George was sitting with his elbow on the window, when the engine hit that rock slide above Appalachian Power Plant at Glen Lyn, Virginia. The impact caught his arm and tore it from his body. When he fell backwards the steam from the engine scalded his whole body. His coffin could not be opened at the funeral. At George's death the Railroad Administration wrote a contract with his widow to assign George's oldest boy to serve as an apprentice, when he became of age.

―◦―

Fourteen years later Harold, 21 years old, showed up for the position at the Railroad. They hired him immediately. After three years of marriage, we were living in Harold's Mother's home and we wanted to start a family. My husband was making two dollars a day as an apprentice. *I wondered why I had not conceived.*

I had severe pains every month and had to stay in bed two or three days. Finally, I went to the doctor and he told me. "There is no way you can conceive because the mouth of the uterus is closed flat and turned back towards your back bone." I asked. "How could that have happened?" He replied. "You must have lifted heavy loads." *I remembered straining myself lifting the drum full of wet clothes out of the Thor Washing Machine. It felt like something pulled in my abdomen. The following month, I had such severe pain I had to go to bed for several days. The Thor washing machine had a large drum with slats in them and about 2 inches apart so the water could circulate as the drum full of clothes circulated over and over. It had a lid to assist in loading the clothes. One day a slat came loose and the drum stopped with the lid on the bottom. I had to lift the drum, full of wet clothes, in order to get to the lid to get those clothes out and finish washing them by hand on a washboard and rinse and wring them out and hang them on the clothesline to dry. The ones I starched, when dry, had to be sprinkled in order to iron them. I thank God for my automatic washer and dryer and all the other appliances we now have today.*

Then the doctor was saying to me, "You will need an operation and maybe then you will be able to conceive."

When my husband came home from work, I told him what the doctor had told me. By the look on his face, I knew he was disappointed. So I told him.

"I don't want to have an operation. If God thinks I will be a good mother He will give us children."

Around the time Fountain Park Skating Rink opened in Oakvale, West Virginia, Georgia drove her big Cadillac from New York to visit the family. When she heard of Fountain Park, she told me.

"Let's go to town and buy us a pair of slacks to go skating."

She drove Harold and me to the skating rink. Once on the floor, I had fear of falling so we went every night so we could practice.

On Saturday night, a friend of Georgia's skated with me while she skated with my husband. After that I felt more sure of my ability to skate without falling.

Sunday afternoon when we arrived at the skating rink, Harold asked me.

"How about you and me skating together?" After four or five times around the rink we were enjoying ourselves and felt confident. I never will know what made us fall but instantly we suffered a hard fall. I fell on my rear and felt a hard jolt and my husband helped me up off the floor. That ended our skating career!

The following month I didn't suffer not one pain and felt like something happened when I fell so hard at the skating rink.

About six weeks later, I missed my monthly and had morning sickness and I knew why. After two months of severe morning sickness, I finally got to feeling better.

When I began having morning sickness, I told my husband. He laughed and said.

"That makes me feel like a man."

Chapter 3

We lived at the edge of town without telephone or a car. One day, a young man at the railroad told my husband.

"I am going to have to turn my 1937, two door sedan Plymouth, back in to Johnson's Motor Company. If Mr. Johnson agrees, would you like to take up my payments?" When Harold told me the payments would be twenty-eight dollars and ten cents a month, I told my husband I didn't know how we would make the payments with our first child on the way. As usual, Harold encouraged me by saying.

"Oh, don't worry about it. There will be a way."

Harold had gotten two free tickets, from the railroad, for us to travel to Katona, to spend Thanksgiving with his mother and family in New York. I decided to make an outfit to wear that would conceal my five month pregnancy. I made a suit of bright pink heavy flannel. To keep my skirt from hiking up in the front, I cut a space below the baby, which went under my stomach. I inserted a draw string around the waist to let out as the baby grew. I wore a heavy black coat, which I had made to wear over it and no one could tell I was expecting. When we were leaving for New York, Harold drove our new car to my parent's house and Father drove us to Bluefield to catch the train.

It was a bright sunshiny day when we left town. When we arrived at Pennsylvania Station there were eighteen inches of snow on the ground. I was happy that I had worn the heavy black winter coat I had made over my new suit. Once in the station, Harold asked which subway we were to take to Katona and the man spoke so fast we didn't understand what he told us. A porter standing nearby told us there would be three transfers to Katona and he offered to go and show us if we paid his five cent fare plus fifty cent fee. That was when I had my first escalator and subway ride. I almost fell, getting on the escalator, and Harold caught me. For all three transfers, each one of us had to put a nickel in the slot of the turntable to pass through the gate to the subway.

When my in-laws saw me they couldn't tell I was pregnant because of the outfit I had made to conceal my condition. However, when I announced that I was expecting, they didn't believe me because the way I was dressed.

"Oh, yes I am! I'm five months pregnant."

The next day the family set out a Thanksgiving turkey dinner and all the trimmings.

The next day we, Harold and me, Harold's mother and sister left Georgia's home and rode the train back to Bluefield where my father met us and drove us to our home on Reed Hill. We were so excited to get home.

My father met Harold and me at the train station in Bluefield and drove us to his home where we had parked our new car. After I got back from New York, I went to the doctor for my monthly checkup and I had gained weight and my blood pressure was up. The doctor gave me a diet to follow and for the next four months I maintained my weight at one hundred and fifty six pounds, which amazed Doctor Frank and his nurse. During the winter I played games with family members, and read 'Gone with the Wind', which my neighbor, Annie loaned me. I also had several visitors.

One time a woman knocked on the door and I invited her in the house and she introduced herself as coming from a church. She began quoting Scripture to me. I had not been to church since getting married and I hadn't read the Bible much. *Whenever I spoke to my husband, about going to church, he would tell me. "I suffered so much sitting in a hot church until I was seven years old. When my father was killed, Mother stopped going to church."* The woman in the living room continued to teach me what she thought the Bible taught and because I showed interest in what she was teaching, she gave me a brightly colored book. It was titled, 'Let God Be True'.

When the woman stood to leave, whom I thought was straight from Heaven, I said.

"Wait just a minute." I went to the kitchen and got her a quart of Green Gage Plums.

"Thank you and God bless you." When I opened the book the woman gave me, the first thing I read, 'There is no burning hell'. When I asked my mother-in-law what she thought about this, she got her Bible and read the Scripture, Luke 16:22-25. *"And it came to pass, that the beggar died, and was carried by the angels into Abraham's bosom. The rich man also died, and was buried, and in hell he lifted up his eyes, being in torment and saw Abraham afar off, and Lazarus in his bosom. And he cried and said, Father Abraham, have mercy on me, and send Lazarus that he may dip the tip of his finger in water, and cool my tongue; for I am tormented in this flame. But Abraham said, Son, remember that thou in thy lifetime received good things, and likewise Lazarus evil things; but now he is comforted, and thou art tormented."* When I heard this Scripture, I took that colorful book, opened the lid on the cooking stove, and threw it in and burned it.

By 1938 most of the family had moved to New York and Harold and I moved from Knob Street to 'Reed Hill', his family home.

Some months later my sister Lena and her husband Bernard came to visit. She told me.

"Mother and one of her friends are going to Nashville, Tennessee, with her preacher and his wife to a General Assembly. Lena and I still had two brothers and two sisters living at home, plus Father still worked in Gary and couldn't watch them. So my sister and her husband and Harold and I spent the week cooking and cleaning while Mother was gone. The job Mother left behind was that she had promised to furnish A & P with twenty-five of her chickens. Our husbands killed the chickens and Lena and I plucked the chickens in a tub of scolding hot water. Then we laid them on a table to remove their insides and then we washed the chickens. We also replaced the liver and neck inside of each chicken according to the store manager and Mother's agreement.

Seven month later, on a Friday at midnight, the first labor pain woke me up and continued throughout my Saturday activities. Since we did not have a telephone I rode with Harold to Bluefield, where Harold had to sign-up for unemployment. The Virginian Railroad was on strike. We stopped at my family's home. Mother cut a slice of peach pie, which I could not eat and that was unusual for me. Mother realized that soon I would be giving birth and gave me some worn-out sheets for the home delivery.

Saturday midnight, the labor pains became worse and my husband drove to the old Princeton hospital for Doctor Fred, father of Doctor Frank, and his nurse, Izetta. When Doctor Fred examined me, he said.

"I am going to give you a twilight shot to relax the womb. The first thing in the morning I am going to have to turn the baby around so the head will be in the right position." The shot put me to sleep. I slept until a labor pain woke me early the next morning, which was Sunday. The doctor and nurse slept at our house. True to his word, the doctor turned the uterus. That was more painful than the labor pains coming hard and fast.

Two hours before the baby arrived, the doctor suggested taking me to the hospital. *He may have thought that I might need to have a cesarean birth.* However, I told him.

"I do not want to go to the hospital." An hour later, I prayed to God.

"I will serve you if you will bring the baby and me safely through this birth."

March 26, 1939, my baby girl arrived screaming. She was nine pounds and nineteen inches long. I named her Janet Marie. I realized immediately I had not asked Harold to suggest a name but he said he liked that name.

Monday morning at work, Harold told C. A. "We have a baby girl born yesterday." Shocked, C.A. answered.

"I didn't know your wife was expecting." Just eight days earlier, we went to the movie with C. A. and his wife. I had worn my designer suit, which I made to conceal my pregnancy. That proved my design successful.

The next Saturday my sister, Lena, delivered a little girl. I wanted to see her baby so badly and for her to see my little girl that I talked my husband into driving me across town to their farm. When Lena saw me she said.

"Shouldn't you have stayed in bed longer." I replied.

"I feel fine and I wanted to see the baby." There were thirteen months between Lena and me. We were mistaken many times as twins, because Mother dressed us alike. We had gone through school together and helped Mother with our four little brothers and sisters. Now we met at Mother's home, with our little girls for Sunday dinners, and our husbands enjoyed being with our Father.

When Janet was two years old, Harold had completed his apprenticeship. He learned that Portsmouth, Virginia shipyard was hiring because they were in production of building ships in case the United States ended up in the war.

We drove to Portsmouth where Harold applied for a job. As soon as his training period with Virginian Railway was finished, instead of waiting to hear from the shipyard, Harold decided to work on the construction of the Radford's munitions plant. The long drive from Princeton, West Virginia to Radford, Virginia, caused my husband to apply to do construction on the Celanese plant. Two weeks after Harold had been working at the Celanese plant a man sitting up in the crane, while Harold worked on the ground, swung a large hook past Harold's head. When my husband looked up, the man was laughing. He swung the hook again, and barely missed his head. Harold saw what he had to deal with and he went straight to the office and resigned.

By now the construction of the Hinton Dam needed workers and Harold hired on as a welder.

A couple of weeks later, Harold's former boss, at the Celanese, wanted my husband to come and work for him at the Appalachian Power Plant, number five unit, in Glen Lyn, Virginia, where he worked until retirement.

Chapter 4

Early spring of 1940, Harold and I were sitting in the swing on the front porch enjoying our little girl, Janet, knowing she would soon have a little sister or brother to play with.

About two months before Juanita was born, my sister Lena and her pretty little girl, Shirley, came to visit Janet and me. Janet was born March 26 and Shirley was born April 1, which made those two little cousins about a week apart. They were both about two years old and loved to play together. While they were busy playing, Lena and me were sitting on the front porch in the swing talking and laughing. I stood up to see what the girls were doing. They were walking just as fast as their little legs could carry them down the driveway. Janet had her potty in one hand and Shirley's hand in the other. They were leaving home in a hurry and Janet made sure to take her potty! Since I was in no condition to run fast to catch them, Lena ran around the house and to the driveway. Suddenly the little girls stopped and started fighting something with their little hands. They had run into a swarm of gnats and that is what slowed them down and made it possible for Lena to catch up with them. We laughed so hard at the little girls, especially Janet, since she thought she was well prepared for anything with her potty.

One evening Harold walked down to the mailbox. He came back holding up a letter from the Draft Board. I figured my husband would have to go fight in World War II. After filling out the questioner, the Draft Board made the decision that Harold's job was necessary to the war effort.

From 1940 to 1941 Germany and Italy, little by little, chipped away at taking control of Continental Europe. During this time, September 2, 1941, since Doctor Frank was still serving in World War II, he had turned his patients over to Doctor Daniel.

While I was giving birth to my second child, Miss Wright administered the ether. I heard Doctor Daniel say, "That felt like too much ether!" My heart stopped; I died! *When I came to the gate of Heaven, the gate keeper shrugged his shoulders and said. "They don't know you! Your name is not written there!" With a sad look on his face, he pointed down; when I looked there, my body was sinking down in a black hole. I cried out with a loud voice! "Too late! Too late! How will I tell Harold and Janet about this?"*

When I opened my eyes, I realized I hadn't died and I breathed a big sigh of relief. *To show God's Grace, God's Riches at Christ's Expense, God still waited for me to come to the knowledge that Christ shed His blood on the cross to redeem me from the bondage of sin.*

This second home delivery was easier because of having gone through it before. When I awoke, the baby girl was already born and weighed over eight pounds and she was nineteen inches long. We named her, Juanita Carol. Everyone crowded around to see the new baby and when Janet came in my bedroom, she walked over to the bassinet. She saw the baby, and she said.

"Oh, ain't it weet. Can I hold her?" Harold told Janet.

"Oh, you can't hold her. I'm afraid you will drop her." I told my husband.

"Put Janet in the big rocking chair. It will be all right."

For the next twelve days, my neighbor, and her son and her sister, were going to live at our house until I resumed my own housework. The ambulance drove her son to the hospital in Charleston, West Virginia, two hours away. When the doctor began an operation on her son's back, he was thinking it was a 'Honey Cone' disease. However, when he discovered the bones were the problem, the doctor closed him up.

Sunday, December 7, 1941, Harold and I put the two girls in the car for our weekly dinner at my parent's home. As I entered the living room, I heard President Roosevelt on the radio saying.

"We declare War on Germany." Father got so excited to see his two granddaughters that he turned the radio off. I said.

"Turn it back on, I heard something important." When he turned the radio back on, President Roosevelt had changed the subject to the Bombing of Pearl Harbor. My family believed that we had to fight back and stop Japan from invading our country.

My youngest sister, Edith 21, announced to the family that she was going to join the Women's Division of the Army, Wac. The recruiters promised her if she joined the Wac she would be able to join her husband, Charles, a Captain stationed in Italy.

The other member of our family, Ed 19 years old, my youngest brother, joined the Merchant Marines. Ed traveled a lot, because he delivered materials to our forces in foreign countries. The day Ed boarded a ship on his way home, a torpedo hit the ship and injured his leg. He spent time in a New York hospital. Edith made the decision not to re-enlist in the service and returned to the family home. The first thing she did was go shopping. She purchased beautiful clothes to wear when she would get to see her husband again. Now that the war was over, everyone wanted to put their lives back together. She received a letter from her husband, Charles. I received a letter from my sister telling me about her husband. The following is an actual paragraph from the letter my sister wrote to me May 14, 1945:

Dear Vera....*I hear from Charles very often any more. I hardly think he wants a divorce, but he's running around with anything and everything with skirts on. He also has a car now. Vera, I've tried my best to talk to him but there's no use. I know he's in love with that girl overseas, so he just will not listen to me. Yet I can't understand him. He says he loves me and it would break his heart to see me marry someone else. What I think is that there has been a mistake made between him and his family and if he only would quit listening to everyone else. I believe with all my heart, Vera, that he's got messed up with that thing overseas and hates to admit it and thinks too much of me to admit it. His conscience is probably hurting him too. I know it would be better if we separate, because if we go back together, it would probably end up in another separation anyway.*

The day Edith went to her in-laws house to wait for Charles to arrive, she looked beautiful. When Charles arrived at his home, he took Edith aside, and told her about his affair with another woman. Then he told her the worse part. "I had to marry her because she got pregnant. Her father would have shot me otherwise.

Now I have to find a house to rent and bring her here to live with me." When my sister heard this news, she ran from the house heartbroken and told our father. He shouted. "CHARLES IS A BIGAMIST WITH TWO WIVES." This made Father very angry and he made an appointment with a lawyer and got this advice.

"It will be very expensive to deal with the overseas legal system."

I had two little girls and I was expecting another baby in six months. Being the oldest child in my family, all of this upset me. Edith was eight years younger, and I raised Edith because my mother was ill from expecting her sixth baby so soon. She had six children in a period of ten years and nine months. I took care of all Edith's needs as a baby. I washed her diapers by hand, fed her, bathed her and put her to bed.

Edith filed for divorce and had to be under a doctor's care. Later she entered 'Little French's Beauty School in Bluefield, West Virginia.

September 1945 my oldest little girl, Janet, started school. Her hair was natural curly. I made long curls hanging around her shoulders. Before Janet's first day at school, I made her and Juanita matching outfits. The morning my first child left to get on the school bus, I felt sad while watching Janet go down the driveway; she looked so sweet and innocent. However, she looked so cute in her outfit I had made her. It was a bright blue wool flannel outfit, with pleaded skirt and had two inch wide straps which came down in front and crossed over on her back. Under the jumper, she had on a white blouse with short puff sleeves and a ruffle around what was called, 'The Peter Pan collar'.

November 20, 1945, Doctor Frank had returned from the War. He didn't arrive at the hospital in time to deliver my third baby girl. Two nurses were assisting me and one gave me ether. *Suddenly, I was standing at the gate of Heaven, again, and expecting the gate keeper to let me in Heaven. The same gate keeper shrugged his shoulders and said, "Your name is not written there; they don't know you." Again he pointed down. I found myself sinking down in a black hole, and I felt the heat coming up. I screamed again. "Too late, too late! How can I tell others?* "When I came to, I realized that I had not died. For the second time, I felt if I experienced this a third time, I would not come back.

I forgot about myself for the joy of having another little girl, Shelby Jean, who weighed eight pounds and she was eighteen inches long. When my husband saw our new baby for the first time, she was lying on a gurney, stark naked, and shivering from the cold. When Harold told me, we were sad together. We couldn't wait to take our little girl and go home.

After three days in the hospital, the baby and I arrived home in an ambulance. First thing, Janet ran to the basinet and said.

"Oh, can I hold her?" However, three year old Juanita felt as if the baby would take her place in the family. She seemed sad when she looked at the baby.

One day Janet came home from school and said.

"Mother, the teacher wants you to make me a hula skirt out of crepe paper for the dance around the May Pole." I cut a waist band to fit my daughter and cut strips of paper up to the waist band and fastened it to the back. The day of the May pole dance, I stood by my car with the window down near my new baby, lying on the seat, watching Janet shake her little hips in the hula dance, which really surprised me. *As I stood there, I reflected back to the first time I had seen her. It was when Harold laid my first born on my chest. I thought, "What a great responsibility I have to raise her right." But later, I thought that she might have inherited some of my husband's love for music and square dancing. When I met Harold he was in a hillbilly band, playing a jug and guitar.*

One Sunday morning I heard the church chimes. It made me feel guilty because I didn't have my children in Sunday school like my mother did for me. I became nervous and agitated and felt I had to work my conviction off by doing the laundry. I was ashamed to hang the clothes outside on Sunday. Instead I hung the laundry in the basement on the lines Harold put up for wintertime. My husband came home from work, walked halfway down the basement steps, saw what I was doing, and he said.

"What in the world are you doing?" I replied. "I'M WASHING CLOTHES. WHAT DOES IT LOOK LIKE?" He yelled back at me. "YOU ACT LIKE SOMEONE CRAZY." I continued.

"I *AM GOING TO BE IF YOU DON'T* GET ME OUT OF HERE AND TAKE ME TO CHURCH." Harold, silently, walked back up the steps.

Mrs. Johns and her daughter brought gifts for the baby one afternoon and there was something special about Mrs. Johns that made me ask.

"What church do you attend?" She told me her church was in Princeton. I continued.

"I would like to get my two oldest girls in Sunday school." My neighbor volunteered.

"I would be glad to come by and take your girls to church." They attended three or four Sundays before my husband had a Sunday off from work. That Sunday I asked Harold if he would go to church with me and he agreed. He drove us to church. Afterwards, we drove home. While fixing Sunday dinner, I told Harold.

"I feel much better." He replied.

"Strange to say, I do too." After a nice Sunday dinner, and playing with our three girls, I asked my husband.

"Will you go back to church with me tonight?" He said.

"Okay, get ready and let's go."

The pastor preached an evangelistic sermon. He gave an altar call and I went up front and got on my knees. When no one came to pray with me, I made a promise to God that night. *"I want to serve You."*

The following Sunday morning, an Evangelist gave her testimony of how happy she was the day she came to know the Lord. She raised her hands and repeated. "I'm saved, I'm saved." The whole church raised to their feet and rejoiced with her.

Monday evening, when Harold came in from work, we sat down at the dinner table.

"Harold, will you say a blessing over the food?" He dropped his head.

"You're the one, not me." *When I was a child my father said the same prayer every meal. I wanted Harold to pray like my father had.* Nevertheless, I repeated my father's prayer with our family.

Most every evening after dinner the family would get in the car and go for a ride, or visit some of the family. The Monday night after Harold and I had attended church the day before, we all got in the car to go for a ride. Harold decided to drive us into the drive-in theater outside of Princeton. The movie was the type I always enjoyed. This night I felt miserable. I was fearful someone from the church would see me. I didn't enjoy the movie at all. Not long after arriving, my husband saw the unhappy look on my face.

"You are not enjoying this, are you?" I replied.

"No, I'm not." Harold started up the car and took us home.

In August of 1948 a small church we could see across the hill from our house, installed a loud speaker on top of their church. It was about a fourth of a mile away from our home. Harold and I sat on the front porch Sunday, listening to the revival music over the loud speaker. We could hear the people shouting and praising God, along with the singing. I asked my husband. "What makes them do that?" Harold replied.

"Well, I remember Grandma Shelley, who had a knot on her jaw. She looked as if she had a jaw breaker in her mouth. We, as kids, would wonder when she would get rid of it. One night we went to church and here came Grandma Shelley. She started walking up and down the aisle shouting!

"LOOK AT MY JAW. PRAISE THE LORD FOR REMOVING THAT GROWTH FROM MY JAW."

For the past nine years, I continuously worried about how to get my name written in Heaven. I knew it had to be done. All I had ever been told was, when I was twelve years old attending the Community church at Wilcoe, that you have to believe Jesus is the Son of God. I, along with the other teens were sprinkled in the name of the Father, Son and Holy Ghost. The pastor told us.

"Now you have the Holy Ghost, go and live a Christian life." However, sitting on the porch with my husband, who had attended a church, where they were allowed to praise God, he gave me insight into what I heard over the loud speaker. After Harold's Father had been killed, working on the railroad, he hadn't been back to any church.

The next morning was the first day of Harold's vacation and we planned two sightseeing trips, one to Shenandoah Valley and on to Washington, DC. Once our luggage was all packed into our new 1947 Plymouth, four door sedan, along with our girls, Janet 9, Juanita 6 and Jean 3 years old, we were on our way.

When we arrived at the Endless Caverns, the girls were excited exploring through the cave. In the ball room I saw a rock shaped like a full size coach, which the guard told me.

"It took millions of years to form." Also other formations in the cavern were mind provoking. *All of this began to make me wonder what the Bible had to say. This caused a desire to come into me to read and study my Bible.*

When we got to Washington, as most tourist, we kept circling in front of the Capitol or going up one-way streets. Once we got to my brother's home, Ed and his wife, we enjoyed a good dinner and went to bed. The next day my brother directed us to the Glen Echo Amusement Park. As we entered the park, we saw a lady in a tall glass cage laughing loudly. She had the appearance, at first, of being real. It got everyone in a good mood, as you could hear her all over the park. I sat on a bench with Shelby Jean, while Harold took Janet and Juanita to ride on the Farris Wheel. Then Harold and Janet challenged each other to the bumper cars.

As I looked at the tall rides, I thought about when I was a young girl and rode the 'Wild Cat' at Coney Island, in Cincinnati, Ohio, in 1937. It was said to have been the tallest in the world. I did not ride any rides at this park, knowing my name wasn't written in Heaven. We arrived back home from our fun vacation Saturday afternoon. That evening after the children were in bed, Harold and I went out to the front porch To our surprise, the revival was still in progress. As we listened to the singing over the loud speaker, I said to him.

"I would like to go and see what is going on there." My husband replied.

"I will take you."

Sunday night, when we arrived at the church, there were no parking spaces left. We drove to the end of the street. As we walked down towards the church, I heard a strange loud noise. I asked my husband.

"What is that noise? He simply answered.

"Sounds like people praying." That scared me and I turned around and started back to the car. Harold took hold of my arm and commented.

"Let's go and see what's going on." Reluctantly, I went on with him. My husband and I entered the church, with three little girls, and sat near the back of the church. After one of the elders of the church and other church members greeted Harold and me, the service began. At this point two men walked to the platform. I learned later one was the pastor and the other was the evangelist. When the congregation began clapping, along with the choir singing, *I thought that was terrible; they should be quiet*. Then the young people started going in and out during the service. I thought they were ill mannered and I felt it was a bad example for my children. When we left the church service, I was determined not to go back to that church.

Monday and Tuesday I kept thinking about two girls, who were praying at different ends of the altar. They began shaking, raising their hands, and praising the Lord at the same time. I had read the Scripture where the Spirit is like the wind. I thought that must be the Spirit of God moving those two girls.

Wednesday morning I called the elder's home, who had treated us so kind, and his son answered. I asked him.

"Is the revival still in progress?"

"No, but there is a prayer meeting tonight and a young people's meeting Friday night." He gave me the complete church schedule.

By the time Harold came home from work, we were dressed and ready to go to prayer meeting. After dinner, he bathed and dressed for church. This evening we sat on the opposite side of the church so my children couldn't see the young people going in and out. They had a visiting pastor from a church in Parkersburg, West Virginia.

After the singing the pastor gave his personal testimony, and at the invitation my husband got up and went to the altar and I followed. For the first time, my husband and I knelt at the altar together. I had never been happier. I felt a joy that I knew my sins were washed away.

After the revival the pastor left for the General Assembly. It was a gathering of pastors for two weeks. He invited another evangelist to come and hold a two week revival.

Sunday morning our family began going to Sunday school and back to worship that night. After church a friend, who knew Harold and I sang, asked if the both of us would sing in the choir during the revival. After Sunday dinner, we rested and went back to church that evening. The evangelist preached a good sermon. At the end of the sermon, I left the choir loft and went to the altar. I got on my knees to seek God. Harold remained seated in the choir on a split-bottom chair. Some young girls were sitting with our daughters on the front row and watching the people rejoice. My husband was watching the people also. He was impressed how happy they were and looked up to the Lord and said.

"Lord, if that is you, I want it." He sat still and waited for his answer from God. He told me later, while meditating on God, he felt something like warm rain coming down over his head and his face. When the gentle rain reached his heart, it began beating real fast. That feeling went all the way down his body and out his feet. He also felt something like nail prints in the palms of his hands and on the tops of both feet. This reminded him of the crucified Christ. That feeling stayed with him all the way home and that night during his sleep his right leg would jerk and wake me up. Neither one of us slept much that night because we were so excited.

The next morning, Harold left for his job at the Appalachian Power Plant in Glen Lyn, Virginia. As soon as he left, the children were still asleep so I went upstairs. I got on my knees and began to pray. I told the Lord.

"I want to train my children in the way you want them to go, as you have said in your Word." I picked up the Bible, Mother had given us when we got married, and opened it to the place where I'd been reading in the New Testament. I read how Jesus had compassion on the afflictions of the people. He made the blind to see, the deaf to hear, and the lame to walk. This said to me, beyond a shadow of a doubt, that Jesus was the Son of God. An ordinary man could not do those works. I realized we were in a good church for us, because the first night we were there a lady testified how the Lord brought her from her death bed so she could raise her children in the faith. She began praising the Lord and spoke in a strange language. *This reminded me of the Scripture: "He that believeth and is baptized shall be saved; but he that believeth not shall be dammed. And signs shall follow them that believe; in my name they shall cast out devils; they shall speak with new tongues;.....They shall lay hands on the sick and they shall recover. So after the Lord spoke to them, he was received up into Heaven and sat on the right hand of God. And they went forth, and preached everywhere, the Lord working with them, confirming the word with signs following. (Mark 16:16-20)*

I looked at the clock. It was time for me to begin my day. When I went downstairs the children were waiting for breakfast. While they ate breakfast I went downstairs and filled my washer with water, added soap powder, and the dirty clothes. I went back upstairs to wash breakfast dishes; waiting until I thought the clothes were clean enough.

I had two square tubs on a stand with rollers, which sat behind the wringer on the washing machine. First I turned off the agitator. I pulled one piece of clothing at a time out of the soapy water. I ran them through the wringer into the first rinse water. Afterwards, I I turned the wringer on the washing machine to extend over the next tub of rinse water. I put the clothes in a laundry basket. I carried the basket up the steps and out to the backyard, where Harold had put two clothes lines on poles. As I hung up those clothes, in the beautiful sunshine and fresh air, I was so happy we had found a good church; I sang and rejoiced. However, in the wintertime washing clothes was a different story. By the time you pulled a pair of long underwear out of the laundry basket, before you could get it hung on the line, it would start to stiffen from the cold. It looked so funny with both legs hanging down stiff.

After working all day Monday, the children and I were ready for the revival by the time my husband got home from work and we ate dinner. The evangelist preached another good sermon. He was a dynamic preacher. After the sermon many people were counseled at the altar by the personal workers. When ladies went to the altar, they were on the left side; men to the right. I went to the ladies side and got on my knees to pray. The personal worker behind me leaned over and said to me.

"Believe the Lord."

Harold and I went every night to the altar. The last night, Harold sat still and didn't go to the altar because a thought came to him. **"You have gone to the altar every night and not received the in-filling of the Holy Ghost. There is no use in**

going to the altar tonight. You will not receive anything." The Scripture came to him: *Even the Spirit of truth; whom the world cannot receive, because it sees him not, neither knows him; but ye know him; for he dwells with you, and SHALL BE IN YOU.* (John 14:17, KJV) He was wanting to receive the Gift that had been promised to believers. After sitting there a few more minutes, he decided.

"I will go to the altar and pray for the sinners, even if I don't receive anything for myself." At the altar my husband knelt to pray over someone. When he paused for a breath, he had praise in his heart for what the Lord had already done for him. Suddenly, Harold felt the same warm feelings come over him. He raised his head and looked up.

"Lord, I believe and receive the Gift of the Holy Ghost." He opened his mouth and waited.

His jaws begin going from side to side. The thought came. **"Look out you'll get lock jaw."** He thought. *"If I get lock jaw, God is able to unlock it."* Knowing his sins were forgiven, Harold continued to yield himself to the Lord. I heard someone say.

"Look at Brother Reed." As I arose from the altar, I saw my husband fall backward in the floor, and it scared me. I had never seen anything like that before. I asked.

"What's wrong with him?" One of the ladies said to me. "He is receiving the Holy Ghost. Go over there and get down beside him and listen." While I was there on my knees, I heard my husband speaking in a strange language. I knew my husband had received the in-filling of the Holy Spirit. Later, he got up from the altar. He looked like he was intoxicated. I was afraid for him to drive the car home. I asked.

"Do you want me to drive?" With slurred speak, he replied very slowly.

"No....I....will...drive". From that evening on, my husband was a changed man. As was usual after dinner, Harold would look for a project to do but now he went to the living room and opened his Bible.

Nannie Reed (Harold's mother) met Gene Morgan and married him. They moved to Princeton, West Virginia and bought a house on Kirk Street. After Grandpa's last job on a tunnel ended he couldn't find another job. Therefore, Harold suggested to his mother and step-dad that they could rent their house and move in our basement apartment until Grandpa Gene could find other work. By fall, he had found another tunnel job and moved to Ronceverte, West Virginia. Over a year later, Grandpa's renters were moving so he and Nannie moved back into their house on Kirk. Once they got settled, they began attending church with our family once again.

Every summer Harold and I planted a large garden. Every evening, after work, my husband helped me in the garden. Also, I weeded the strawberry patch, while my husband was at work, and Janet watched the girls. I wanted a rock garden, so I gathered good sized rocks in a wheelbarrow. Then my husband helped me by bringing large sized rocks from the mountain for the backdrop of the garden, and in front of it I planted tea cup size and a variety of colored tulips.

Later that week, I picked beans while my husband was at work. I carried jars from the basement and washed and rinsed them in hot water. I drained them and to sterilize them, I placed them in a real warm oven until I was ready to use them. I did the same thing for making tomato juice and canning vegetables from the garden. I canned 28 quarts of green beans that day. I cleaned my kitchen, and was getting ready to go to bed, when Grandpa Gene arrived with a large three gallon zinc bucket of blackberries. The kitchen was still hot from canning all day. My family was in bed asleep.

I was afraid the berries would spoil overnight; I washed them and began again until almost midnight. There was usually someone to pick vegetables for me in the evening so I could get an early start in the morning. After washing the tomatoes, I cut them in quarters, placed in a large pot and cooked them until soft. Afterwards, I placed them in a cone shape colander. Then I took a cone shape maul made of hard wood, which I turned around and around to press the juice out of the tomatoes and added a teaspoon of sugar and salt to each quart before canning.

One time we went to church and I dreamed afterwards. *I saw this orange crate between my bed and window. I could see snakes in the crate. I started to go over and lift the lid when a voice said. "Don't bother them."* That woke me up. That was a strange dream.

Then I heard about a revival about twenty minutes away in the coal fields and my husband agreed that we could attend. As we walked up the aisle our feet left foot prints in the thick coal dust. After the singing and preaching, the evangelist gave an altar call. I and my friend, who was very particular, went forward and stooped down instead of letting our knees touch the floor because we did not want to get our good clothes dirty. When my friend tapped me on the arm and whispered.

"There's a big black spider!" Together we both stood up and I looked for Harold. My friend replied.

"I think he is over there among that group of people; we walked over there. When I saw my husband lying flat on his back in that brand new dark tan custom made suit, I thought. *Surely his suit is ruined and his head is in coal dust and I just know he will look like a coal miner when he stands up.* Then I realized my husband was being blessed by God. When he stood up he looked intoxicated again. However, he had a glow on his face. At night, Harold would always kneel on his side of the bed and I knelt on my side. I had tears in my eyes because I desired the same kind of relationship with the Lord. The day after the revival I called the dry cleaners and there was no damage to my husband's suit.

※

That September, when school began, Janet would be in third grade and Juanita was starting first grade. I put matching dresses on them and stood on the front porch watching them walk down the road. I was thinking. *I'm glad that Shelby Jean is still asleep, because she would cry if she saw Juanita leaving with Janet.* I had a time fixing the two girls hair for school. Their hair was so different. Juanita's hair wouldn't hold a curl so I parted it in the middle in the back and made a French plait on each side. Janet's hair was easier and I made long curls all around her head. When Shelby Jean woke up, I told her that Juanita had started to school with Janet. Then I gave her a hug and kiss and told her.

"When you get old enough you will be going to school with Janet and Juanita." That seemed to comfort her.

When the weather got cooler, I purchased school clothes for the girls. I bought them just alike, only in different colors so they would know their clothes. I bought Buster Brown shoes for both and more material to make dresses alike.

Instead of going out 'trick or treating' I made a jack o' lantern for the front porch, popcorn balls and ginger bread men with faces, for treats. Harold was off from work on Saturdays and would take the family for rides through the mountains to see the beautiful colored leaves. They would begin to dry up by Thanksgiving. Our many trees dropped enough leaves in our yard for the girls to wade through the leaves and cover each other up.

As Christmastime got near, I began decorating the house with lights around the front porch and on the hemlock tree. I left the lights on the tree during the years and as the tree grew a foot or more by the next Christmas, I would add another row of lights below the first row and by the time the hemlock was about nine feet tall, I took a step stool to add another row of lights to the last row. All the neighbors missed that tree when the state road built a highway through our neighborhood.

By Christmas I had my fresh ham boiling with onions. When the girls went to bed, Santa set out each girl a doll, table games, clothes and Christmas candy. Harold purchased a three foot standing elephant with weights in the bottom. When the girls punched the elephant it would go to the floor and back. They had a lot of fun with that toy.

After Harold received the Holy Ghost, one Sunday morning in church, I heard the teacher telling in detail the crucifixion of Jesus Christ when he pointed his finger at me and continued.

"It was for YOU he died." When he said that, my heart began beating fast with the knowledge that Jesus died for ME, and he's now my own personal Savior. A great love came into my heart and I desired to draw closer to Jesus.

All winter I continued to pray and seek God for the Gift that my husband had received. The following June my two little girls, Juanita and Shelby Jean, began with a whoop in their cough and they were throwing up. I took them to Doctor Daniel. He told me. "I'm sorry to tell you; your daughters will cough until the leaves fall in the fall because they have taken this disease after the leaves came out in the spring." I stood shocked as he continued. "Be glad they didn't take it in the fall, after the leaves fall, because they would cough all winter until the leaves come out in the spring."

After that my husband called our Pastor to come out to pray for our daughters because they had whooping cough. The Pastor replied. "I'll be honest with you Brother Reed, two of my children had whooping cough. We prayed for them and the church prayed. I even called our general office and they did not get healed. Therefore, I feel it's not much use to pray for your daughters to get well before its time."

When Harold told me what the Pastor said, I went straight to the telephone and called to ask my mother. "Do you think God can heal whooping cough?" She said, "Why Vera, God can do anything that we believe him for." After my mother's encouragement I went to the bedroom where my husband sat with the girls. I looked at my husband and said. Jesus says, ". . . *These signs shall follow them that believe.....*"

"Harold, you have already received the Gift and by faith you should be able to lay hands on the sick, and they shall recover. My husband laid his hands on our two girls and prayed for them in other tongues. I knew that the Holy Ghost prayed for them. I also knew that the prayer of the Holy Ghost is always answered. We raised our hands, praised the Lord for his goodness, grace and the word. We kissed our precious little girls goodnight and went to bed. For the first time in two weeks, I got a good night's sleep because the girls cough had ceased.

The next morning the fever was gone. There was no more coughing and the container sitting beside the bed for the girls to use, if they had to throw-up, was dry. They were healed completely. That evening we decided, since the girls were healed, we would go to the revival at church. Because of our concern that people would think we were spreading the whooping cough germ, Harold parked the car near the entrance of the church. My husband and I went in to the revival, and he checked on the girls often. After the church service, as Sister Susie was leaving the church she saw the girls sitting in the car and asked them.

"Have you girls been sitting out here in the car throughout church?" Janet said.

"Yes." I added.

"We were afraid to take them in for fear someone would think we are spreading whooping cough. Our girls were healed last night when my husband prayed over them."

"Sister Reed, I know they are healed because I have seen all kinds of diseases healed. Now tomorrow night you bring those girls in the church."

Chapter 5

Our Pastor invited evangelists almost every week during the summer. I invited my father and mother to every one of the meetings. They decided to attend Evangelist Billy and Jean's two week revival every night. However, the last night of the revival, I knelt at the altar. My Pastor touched me on the shoulder and said.

"Look who is beside you Sister Reed." I wasn't surprised to see Father there because my husband had been praying for him. Mother had gotten saved years before, and now I looked into my father's face to see peace. I knew he had just gotten saved.

My pastor saw so many coming to the altar to accept Jesus Christ, he ask the evangelists to hold the revival for another week. Mother told me later, when Father got home he emptied his cigarette jar in the stove with a carton of cigarettes I had given him. He further washed the jars in the smoke stand and told Mother.

"With God's help, I intend not to smoke anymore." And he didn't. After that my parents were active in church until they objected to members selling their wares among the congregation inside the sanctuary, to raise money for the church. One Sunday as my mother went out the door, there stood a woman selling. My mother made the comment.

"Don't you know it's a sin to sell in the church?" The pastor overheard my mother. The next day he telephoned her and said.

"I didn't appreciate you causing division in my church. The best thing for you to do is to stay home." The pastor didn't think about my father being a new convert and hungry to know more about God. My parents were left without a church and my father a new Christian without a teacher.

As a child I had seen my father reading the Bible most every evening after dinner. Later he and mother began attending a church close to their home. The first thing the pastor did was to put Father in as adult Sunday school teacher. He knew my Father had read his Bible for over sixty years. After getting saved at 60 years old, my father understood the Scriptures like never before. The last night of the revival at my church, a new family was visiting. They introduced themselves as Mr. and Mrs. Hall. They had two little girls. They invited our family to come to their home for a visit. We felt it would be all right to go, since we met them at church, and our pastor seemed impressed with them. Mr. Hall had given a powerful testimony for God. To my husband and me the family seemed like good people. When we arrived at their home, their landlady had locked the door and ordered them to leave. Their two little girls were blue with the cold and shivering in the real cold weather. Harold and I felt sorry for that family because that could be us and our three girls. I suggested that the family gather what they needed from the house and we would make a place for them in our basement.

The next evening, Mr. Hall stopped at the country store, and unknown to us, he opened a charge account. He brought home a large beef roast for dinner. Harold feared Mr. Hall would run up a large account and would not be able to pay. As near as we could figure, this is what happened: Mr. Hall had a great fear of working in the mines. This caused him to miss so much work and he could not pay his bill at the store. Once the Hall family settled in our home his wife packed a large stack of sandwiches the day her husband was going to return to the mines. I asked Mrs. Hall.

"Why do you pack so many sandwiches?" She replied.

"Well, my husband wants enough sandwiches in case the roof of the mines cave in on them. He wants to make sure there is enough to eat." Mr. Hall went out every day. We didn't know if he went to work or not, until one day his wife confessed that her husband had quit the mines. He went out every morning looking for another job.

The incident that caused me to lose confidence in Mr. Hall was one Sunday afternoon we were all setting in the living room and he asked.

"Do you have something for a headache?" I gave him a Stanback Headache Powder. About an hour later, my father and mother arrived for a visit and during the conversation Mr. Hall began giving his testimony.

"I'll tell you, our God can do anything. We serve a great God and He can even heal a headache." He overlooked the fact that I had just given him something to take for his headache!

Mrs. Hall and her girls were getting along fine with me and my girls.

To petition off the rooms in the basement for this family, Mr. Hall volunteered to hang the wallboard for rent and he went to the Virginian Supply to purchase nine sheets of wallboard on our charge account.

When the building supply delivered the wallboards, there were ten. After the delivery man left, I asked.

"Why did you to get ten." Mr. Hall replied.

"I knew he was giving me ten and I felt like the Lord was blessing us."

Harold had suspicions that Mr. Hall had run up a high bill at the country store. My husband and I had secret talks with each other about this situation. One thing I had become concerned about was leaving my three girls while we went to get groceries. I told my husband.

"I don't believe we can trust him." He said.

"I'll tell you what we have to do is lock the door to the basement before we leave so he can't get upstairs." The straw that broke the camel's back was, one night I was going to the basement for a jar of preserves. Halfway down the steps, I heard Mr. Hall talking to his wife.

"I went and talked to the Pastor and told him about all those filthy magazines Sister Reed has stacked on a shelf in her closet." Mr. Hall had gone to our upstairs bedroom and found in a walk-in closet: True Stories, True Confessions, True Romance, and Detective Magazines. My sister had given those to me when we were younger. Over the years I forgot they were there. The day that Harold went into the country store, the owner confided that our free boarders had run up a large charge account. He asked my husband.

"What about Mr. Hall? Is he working? He has bought all this food and never paid a cent on his account." My husband commented.

"I can't recommend him and I wouldn't let him charge anything else."

The next Sunday the pastor began his sermon on, 'Restitution after Salvation'. He told about an alcoholic that got saved and stopped drinking. One of the man's neighbors saw a bottle of whiskey sitting on a shelf behind the door and asked.

"If you're saved and have stopped drinking, why is that bottle of whiskey behind the door?" The saved alcoholic looked and saw the bottle and answered.

"Oh, I forgot about that bottle of whiskey." He poured it down the drain. The pastor ended that example with these words.

"You need to clean the shelf behind the door." On the way out the door I faced my pastor and made the comment.

"I'm going home and clean my shelf off." The next day I took the entire stack of magazines outside to burn. Within days Mr. Hall informed us they would be moving nearer to the church. My husband replied in a stern voice.

"I think that would be a good idea."

Years later, Mrs. Hall's sister told me, the Halls divorced. I asked.

"Why did they divorce?" She shared with me.

"One day Mrs. Hall came home from work and found Mr. Hall with their twelve year old daughter. Harold and I learned a great lesson. *Be cautious around people we know nothing about.*

Chapter 6

Norma started to our church from a church nearby. The first time she went to the altar she received the gift of the Holy Ghost.

I was thinking. *I have been seeking the Lord for eleven months and have not received the Gift.* I told Norma,

"I don't know why I haven't received the Holy Ghost." She told me.

"Sister Reed, you need to go down to the altar determined." I told her.

"I don't have the faith to receive." Norma answered.

"Ask the Lord to give you the faith. The Holy Ghost is a light. When you get down on your knees look for the light. Keep your mind on it and believe. Stay there until you receive the Holy Ghost, regardless of how long it takes."

The next morning I went upstairs, determined to receive the faith for this wonderful Gift. I picked up my Bible and read. *The Holy Ghost is given to those who believe and obey God. I looked* up and prayed. *"Lord, what would you have me do?"* The names of three people popped into my mind and the Lord told me to write them a letter and tell them what happened to me. I got up and went to my desk and began writing. *I have been saved and I'm seeking God for the baptism of the Holy Ghost, according to Acts 2:4."* To all three, I apologized for something that happened during the years in high school and I asked them to forgive me. When I got all three letters ready to mail, I went back and knelt down and asked the Lord. "Now that I have all three letters ready to mail, what else would you have me do?" I waited for His answer. Then I felt the faith come into me and it made me feel alive, like I had never felt before. It seemed like it saturated my whole body. I felt a Holy presence of God that made me afraid to move.

All day long I had that same feeling. I believe God had a purpose for me to wait until that night. I didn't want to disturb the presence of God but I had to go to town to pay my light bill and go to the grocery store. I went to the check-out at the A&P. There was the same girl who had asked me several days before.

"Why do you stay at the church so late?" I had told her at that time.

"People are waiting upon God around the altar to receive the baptism of the Holy Ghost according to Acts 2:4."

When she began checking out my groceries, we didn't talk. She just stared at me, which puzzled me. I wondered if the way I was feeling showed in my face, but neither of us mentioned anything. When I got home I put my groceries away. I cooked dinner for the family and I anxiously went to dress for church. Being preoccupied with that night's service, I had very little to say to the family.

Thursday night I arrived at church with my family. After being greeted by the people, I noticed they stared at my face. Harold and I went up front and sat down with the choir until time for the service. Our pastor reintroduced the evangelist as the speaker for the revival. The evangelist gave Scripture proving the need for receiving the Holy Ghost. Ephesians 1:12-14: *In whom you also trusted, after that ye heard the word of truth, the gospel of your salvation: in whom also after that ye believed, you were sealed with that Holy Spirit of promise, which is the earnest of our inheritance until the redemption of the purchased procession, unto the praise of His glory."*

After the message, when the singing began, I went to the altar. While kneeling there I told the Lord.

"I need the baptism of the Holy Ghost to teach me how to raise my children according to your will. I also want this Gift to have power for service to work for you and win souls; now I present my body a living sacrifice."

After standing up, I raised my hands to the Lord and thanked Him for the free gift of salvation.

I had been embarrassed every time I fell in the floor under the power of God. I deliberately went to my knees and stretched out my body as a living sacrifice to the Lord.

I lay on the floor three hours with both hands straight up in the air waiting for the Holy Ghost to come in. I remembered John 14:17 .....*for the Holy Spirit dwelleth with you, and shall be in you."*

After most of the people went home, my parents and prayer warriors continued to kneel on each side of me, praying. My husband told me later, my parents stayed until eleven before going home.

I received the Holy Spirit at eleven-forty-five. As I continued to lie on the floor, I felt impressed to say, "Glory, Glory, Glory," *with my mind thinking of the light Norma had told me to look for. As I* continued to say, "Glory, Glory, Glory." This thought came to my mind. **If you don't stop saying it, you will die,** but I continued. The word, reach, came to me. I reached as high as I could. I saw the light coming and it landed on my forehead. Then my tongue got loose and I began speaking in tongues. My voice sounded like a strange train whistle and joy unspeakable flooded my soul. I began to laugh. I laughed and laughed. "...*Jesus Christ: Whom having not seen, ye love; in whom, though now ye see him not, yet believing, ye rejoice with joy unspeakable and full of glory."*

About midnight Harold helped me up off the floor. The children were stretched out on the bench sound asleep. Somehow, my husband got my girls awake and all of us in the car. I laughed all the way home.

Early the next morning, I called my parent's home and told Father I had received the in-filling of the Holy Ghost. I received on Thursday night. Monday, while I was wringing my clothes in the rinse water, I began thinking. *I am a changed lady from the last time I washed clothes in this washing machine.* Before that, I had taken for granted that my husband had gone out of his way to make everything handy for me to wash. Now I began to praise and thank God for all that my husband had done for me. I was filled with more love for my husband, working every day making a good living for the family, plus the help he gives me with the girls. I had a great respect for my husband for yielding himself to the Lord and receiving the baptism of the Holy Ghost and taking his place as head of our home. Now my husband never failed to ask the blessing over our meals and make intercession in prayer for others. As I washed and hung out the laundry, I sang hymns and rejoiced in the Lord.

One Monday morning hanging out laundry and rejoicing, a pressing need to pray came upon me. I lifted my hand and began praying earnestly, making intercession for something I didn't know about. However, I knew the prayer of the Holy Spirit would be answered.

At dinnertime that evening I saw a strange look on my husband's face and he wasn't eating very much. I asked.

"Harold, are you all right?" He finally opened up and told me.

"I am thinking of how near I came to not being here this evening. I was in a tight place in a boiler. I was mirror welding a ruptured tube. I suddenly felt the immediate need to get out of there. The smoke was so strong I couldn't breathe. I jumped down into the main department and there stood my boss and helper. I shouted.

"GET OUT OF HERE QUICKLY." I began to see the whole place fill with dense smoke, which was so strong that it took our breath. I knew that neither of the men, that was there with me, had a relationship with God. I didn't want them to die in there. Afterwards, when I got in the room where they had been, the smoke was so dense, I couldn't see where to walk. Choking on the smoke, a voice in me was saying. *"Lay down flat on your stomach." Landing on my stomach, my face* landed near an air vent and I breathed fresh air from the outside. Men with masks arrived to take me to the outside. I was thankful to be breathing fresh air on the outside.

The urge for me to pray had come from the Holy Spirit. I was praying for Harold at the same time of the accident. I appreciate the presence of the Holy Ghost in our lives as our Helper. One morning, I awoke with swelling on the left side of my neck. My husband saw that it was so red and throbbing me. He said.

"I am staying home from work and taking you to the doctor." I decided to wait until later in the day to see if the swelling went down in my neck.

By the time Harold came home from work, there was no sign of the swelling and all pain had stopped. Some people thought I was foolish for not going immediately to the doctor. Not long after that I had my foot on my husband's side of the bed and his large toenail made a scratch above my heel on the leg. It hurt but, being so sleepy, I went back to sleep. The next morning, the pain from that scratch woke me. When Harold came home from work and had his dinner, because he had blood poison as a child, he wanted the doctor to check the spreading infection on the back of my leg. However, we were in revival with missionaries that evening and I wanted the people in church to pray for me. Nevertheless, my husband scared me into going to the doctor and having the scratch checked. The doctor left the room to take a telephone call and left me sitting in his office. The words came in my mind while waiting for the doctor, *You are not the same person you were the last time you were in this office.* I thought. *No, I'm now saved and have been filled with the Spirit.* Then this thought. "If you had asked me, I would have healed you." Then I realized I had not asked the Lord once that day to heal the back of my leg. When the doctor returned he told me I had a dangerous infection, which spreads fast. Afterwards, he gave me a prescription for a new type of antibiotic.

When I got home I wanted to ask God to heal me but my husband handed me a glass of water and a pill, which I had to swallow. The pill stuck in my throat. I slipped in the bathroom and flushed the pills down the commode.

The next morning, I told my husband I did not take the pills. After he left for work, I went upstairs to the prayer room. I reminded the Lord He said He would heal me if I ask Him. I remained there for a while praying and praising the Lord. When my husband came home from work that evening, he asked.

"How is the infection in your leg?" Together, we took the bandage off my leg and the three girls were anxiously watching. All we saw was a red scar.

As the girls were growing up they were trained to help in the summertime with the chores. Janet, being the oldest, stayed in the kitchen to help me with the canning. I would send Juanita and Shelby Jean to the garden to pick green beans and together we strung the beans.

Other things the girls liked to do were, run and play in the orchard next to us, and their music.

Mrs. Summers taught all three of the girls to play the piano. One afternoon Janet took her hymnal to piano practice and asked Mrs. Summers.

"Will you teach me how to play hymns?" The teacher replied.

"We have to finish the lessons in the workbook before school is out." That day my oldest daughter came home disappointed. I tried to comfort her when I said.

"Don't worry about it. The Lord is able to help you play." That same evening, washing dinner dishes, I heard a different sound coming from the piano in the living room. I dried my hands and walked into the living room. When she reached the end of the song, she turned around and asked.

"Mother can you write real fast?" It took my daughter three times before I got all the words written on the paper. I looked at her, with tears in her eyes and her face all aglow with the presence of the Lord, and I said to her.

"Janet, I told you the Lord would help you." Joyfully, she replied.

"I want to use this gift to play hymns in church."

One afternoon the girls were sitting on the front porch singing. There was a man under the house building a rock wall and heard them. When I went to pay him for the work, he made a comment.

"You got some good little singers sitting up there on the porch." Before Janet began playing the piano publicly, as a girl of twelve, she would hear different people play in church and they would add extra notes, which gave Janet the desire to play hymns like they did.

When the girls were young, and we only had one car then, Harold and I went grocery shopping on Saturday mornings while the girls stayed at home. While we were gone to the store they were actually practicing singing together after they finished their chores. Janet sang the alto and Juanita and Shelby Jean were singing the lead. However, Janet had such a low voice that I wouldn't have dreamed that the girls could ever harmonize together.

It was at a young people's service before Easter, when we first heard the girls sing together. When the announcer stood up and said.

"Janet and her sisters are going to sing." My mind began spinning and thinking. *Oh my goodness! Janet and the girls can't harmonize.* Harold and I were shocked when they began harmonizing and afterwards the congregation gave them a round of applause. An elder in the church pointed his finger at the three girls and announced.

"The Reed Sisters are going to sing together."

As they grew older, we traveled around the area to other church revivals. There were requests for the Reed Sisters to sing.

One Sunday the Reed Sisters were invited to sing at the newly built Painters Chapel. Harold had to work that Sunday and I drove the girls to Lerona, West Virginia. At the end of the service, I waited on the girls out on the small porch, about 12 x 14, which had five or six steps down to the ground. When we were leaving people stopped to congratulate me on the girl's singing. Gradually, in acknowledging the people, unknown to me, I stepped backwards and closer to the edge of the porch. When almost everyone had left, suddenly, from behind a man's arms wrapped around my waist and lifted me up and stood me down on the ground. As soon as he lifted his hands, I immediately, turned around to thank him and I couldn't see a sign of anyone. Where did he go and where did he come from, since there were so few people left. I realized when I looked where I was and where I would have fallen, I thought. *Was that my guardian angel that caught me and sat me on the ground so I wouldn't break my neck? I was* embarrassed and looked to see if anyone saw me; I knew they would be laughing. Then I saw some men standing and talking on the other side of the steps and they obviously hadn't seen a thing because the men weren't looking in my direction.

The Mercer County Singing was for anyone who wanted to sing. It was held once a month at different places, such as in the courthouse. The Sunday the Singing was held at our church, our family arrived fifteen minutes early. The hillbilly singers came in and sat in front of us. Suddenly, one of the hillbillies took a bottle out of his pocket. Jason leaned over and whispered to me.

"I hope that's cough syrup."

Every year in June, our State Camp Meeting was held in Beckley, West Virginia. The meeting attracted many different musical groups. The Reed Girls were a popular singing trio and the music director had them on the agenda to sing. The Reed Girls were always asked to sing so they were always learning new songs in their practice sessions at home.

Even though I was a woman, I felt the call upon my life to preach. One day I got a call from Pastor Nelson asking if I would preach a revival at his church starting Sunday night?

On one occasion this pastor had given me good advice. I was going through a trial and the pastor told me. "You are going to have to learn how to let these ugly remarks roll off your back like water off a duck's back." I replied, "How do you do that?" The pastor remarked. "Forgive them because of their ignorance. Then you ask the Lord to bless them, and turn it over to the Lord and forget about what was said." I told Pastor Nelson that morning when he called.

"I already have the first sermon."

Sunday night when I arrived at the church and saw those high school young people, I felt their need of the Lord. Brother Nelson introduced the Reed Girls and after they sang, I went to the pulpit to speak on Salvation.

My family and I always got to the church early. I went in and sat down on the end of the back pew waiting for the people to gather. Here comes a man through the door and went down front and hugged all the men. I thought. *"Good, here is another godly man that can help at the altar as a personal worker."* The Lord revealed to me.

"He is a sinner." I had a hard time believing this about the man until I stood up to speak. This man began speaking in a strange language. It was obvious that his goal was to break up the meeting. Brother Nelson went over and sat beside him and put his arm around his shoulder. The man didn't appreciate the pastor keeping him quiet. After the sermon people came to the altar to pray. I heard the man tell the pastor.

"I'm sure that was God using me." Brother Nelson told the man.

"No you were keeping our speaker from giving out her sermon. If that's the way you are going to act during this revival, I don't want you to come back." We were in a country church where people had not been taught how to act.

The next thing that happened was, two big teenage boys came and stretched out on a pew up front. The next night they did the same thing and pretended to be asleep. This happened for three nights in a row. The fourth night the Lord reminded me of the history of the people, when they first started to worship in this country. They also encountered such problems as sleeping in church. I told them that the Word of the Lord is so important to listen to that when the pilgrims came over and landed at Plymouth Rock, the first thing they did after they got settled, was to build a meeting house where they preached the word, prayed and worshiped God. They preached so long that some of the people would go to sleep. They solved the problem by sitting a man on a high stool in the corner. He would take a long fishing pole and on the end of the line would be a rock. Every time he saw someone nodding off he would tap them on the head with the rock to wake them up. After learning about that, the two teenage boys sat up straight and listened. As fate would have it, the timing of a horrible tragedy came during the revival. Sunday afternoon, a local woman had been to church and for some reason her car left the highway and went into Wolf Creek to the deepest part. The woman in the front seat and her two sons in the backseat all drown; she was the aunt to the two teenage boys who slept through my sermons. Brother Nelson asked me.

"Should we close the revival?" I replied.

"I don't know, what do you think?" He said.

"I believe we should close the revival until after the funeral."

"Why don't we meet here for prayer Friday night after the funeral?"

When the revival began again on Friday night, we prayed and, I brought another sermon. Sunday night Janet stood up from the piano and said.

"I need prayer." The young people began going to the altar. The timing of the tragic accident let the young people see how fast their life could be snuffed out. Pastor Nelson, his wife, Harold and I, were watching the young people pray and accept Jesus. Suddenly my twelve year old, and the pastor's daughter, knelt at the altar with their little hands up in the air. My heart jumped for joy when the two teenage boys came to the altar that had slept through my sermons, to receive Jesus as Lord. When I agreed to hold the revival, I didn't know it would last for seven weeks.

A woman came to me after her son got saved at the altar. She, very rudely, said to me. "I don't believe what you're teaching. She proceeded to tell me.

"You're teaching 'Jesus only' doctrine. We're not saved by the blood; we're saved by the church." Kindly, I suggested.

"You go home and look up all the Scriptures on the blood." Pastor Nelson also went home and looked up the Scriptures on the blood. The next night he stood and shared.

"I went home last night, looked up the Scriptures on the blood and found out that we are really saved by the blood of Jesus." Most of the young people that came to the altar went back to the church and brought a friend to hear the Gospel. The next Sunday, Brother Nelson invited Harold and me to attend the baptizing of twenty people after that revival!

Chapter 7

The next summer, the girls were swinging on the porch when suddenly they began screaming.

"Mother, Mother." I went running to see what had happened. They were pointing to a snake that looked about six feet long, lying on the ground close to a tree. The garden had just been plowed, out from that tree. By the time I came around the house with my hoe, the snake had crawled out on the plowed field. I began running up and over the furrows. I was close behind, with a hoe in my hand, chasing him over the furrows and through the garden. When the snake stopped crawling, he was under an apple tree, and his tail lay over the bank in front of me. I raised the hoe up and then down across his tail. He wheeled around and began chasing me. I was wearing Harold's baggy white shirt and with shirt tails flying and a large straw hat on my head, I ran for my life back towards the house. When I arrived, my three girls were laughing. I looked back and didn't see the snake.

That evening I told my husband about the snake. He became concerned and told me. "An injured snake can be dangerous and I'm going after it." I followed my husband, carrying the hoe, so I could help him. *I remembered Harold was far-sighted. He could see at a great distance. One day he looked over on an opposite hill and saw a bear. I couldn't see it and he said. "Don't you see the bear? He's standing up."* Now he was asking me.

"Do you see that snake coiled around the branch on that tree?" I didn't. He said.

"I'm going to rock it out of the tree. Hand me all the rocks you can find." Again he asked.

"Do you see the snake on the ground?" I didn't. Shortly after that incident I realized how badly I needed glasses.

The Harvey family, Lula, Gene, Denny, Gary and Penny were going to move to Birmingham, Alabama. Lula asked me.

"Could my three children stay a couple of weeks with you while we renovate our house?" I told her.

"I would be glad for them to stay and be company for my girls."

The day Lula and Gene were leaving, their son Gary came around the house wearing his mother's corset laced up in the front as tight as he could get it and twisting his hips like a model. He stood in front of our fishpond posing. His mother shouted. "I'M GOING TO GET YOU GARY." He took off running back in the house. Everyone was laughing hard and the parents shouted to their three children. "MIND YOUR MANNERS"

For the next two weeks the six children ran and played outside. At night they played games and sang as Janet played the piano. We all went to church on Sundays and Wednesday nights. I cooked meals for the children with good desserts. At the end of two weeks, we were sad to say goodbye to our friends.

After the family moved, we were invited to spend a week as their house guests in Birmingham. The children were excited to be back together again and I enjoyed being with Lula. We went sightseeing, going to the zoo, going to church and to visit her family. The most unusual was the fig trees in their backyard. Lula told us in the springtime the trees had little knobs on the branches, which turn out to be the figs and then the leaves came out. We had our first fig preserves for breakfast and delicious fried okra for dinner.

When we got back home, I invited our church family to our home for a cookout. One family brought blueberry pies to add to our grilled hamburgers and chili slaw dogs. But the funniest part of the evening was, my friend kept sticking her blueberry tongue out and she painted a mustache on her lips.

In September Janet began her freshman year in high school, Juanita was in seventh grade and Shelby Jean began her third year of school. The hardest part of school starting, was Juanita's birthday on September 2. I always made each family member a cake on their birthday. I would be so busy getting my three girls in school, making school clothes, buying shoes, and buying school books that I didn't have time to make Juanita a birthday cake.

I awoke one morning, with my brother Otie on my mind. I began to pray for him, thinking there might be a need. Harold had awakened and was praying in the Spirit.

The next evening I called Mother and she told me.

"Otie and his wife and baby are here with us." Our family went to visit them. Otie sat down beside me on the couch and began to tell me what happened that morning about four o'clock.

"We were on our way to Princeton to visit Mother. I was playing tag with another car, when all of a sudden I must have went to sleep and I woke up to find my front wheels were hanging over a guardrail and the car was about to go over a steep bank. The man who had been playing tag with me, called for a wrecker to pull me out. I was afraid to move or even try to get out of the car. His wife interrupted.

"That was one time I prayed." I looked over at my husband and we both understood why God had led us to pray that morning. Harold said to my brother.

"I see now why the Holy Ghost woke both of us up to pray this morning."

I began to think of all the things that happened to Otie when he was a young boy. I ask him.

"Do you remember the time you came home with blood running down from your head and Mother was about to faint?" I told Lena.

"You take care of Mother and I will take care of Otie." I sat him down and applied a damp cloth to his head to stop the bleeding. I took Father's razor and cut his hair from around the wound. He told me, he and a friend where skipping rocks across the river and as he rose up from picking up a rock, his friend threw one and hit him in the head. The deep cut would have to be stitched. When father came home from work, he drove Otie and me to the doctor. The doctor asked.

"Who cleaned this wound?" My father said.

"My daughter cleaned it." The doctor looked at me and told me I did a good job and would make a good nurse. I always thought I wanted to be a nurse, until I took a business course in high school, and then I wanted to work in an office.

I asked Otie about another time, when he was gone all day.

"Suddenly we heard a strange noise on the pavement. A boy brought you home in a wheel barrow. You boys had been playing in the river. When you came out of the water, you saw white ashes on the ground and when you stepped in the white ashes, there were red hot coals still burning under them." Once in the ashes, it was a long distance to walk out of the fire. Otie burned the bottom of his feet and his ankles. He was forced to stay home, since he couldn't walk.

"Otie, remember the time we were cleaning out a closet upstairs and you reached down in a box to pick up a shoe and a mouse ran up your sleeve. You grabbed that mouse and was squeezing it and jumping up and down screaming? I kept telling you.

"Let loose of it. You will squeeze it to death, but you wouldn't let loose of it until I made you understand. You finally believed me and let the mouse loose and it fell to the floor dead.

"Now take that sweater off and I will wash it for you."

"Otie, somehow you always had black coal dust on your feet. You would come home tracking it on the clean carpets and in your bed." One day Mother had enough and told him.

"Otie, I am putting a bucket of soapy water on the back porch with a towel and you are to wash your feet and dry them before coming into this kitchen." However, the first day after that, Mother forgot to put the soapy water on the porch for his foot washing.

"When you arrived home, there was a bucket of sweet milk with foam on top sitting on the table. It looked like soapy water. Do you remember sitting that bucket of milk down on the floor and washing your feet and then you sat the bucket back upon the table?" When Mother came out to strain the milk, she shouted!

"WHAT ARE THESE BLACK STREAKS IN THE MILK?"

"Then she realized that she had forgotten your bucket of soapy water and you had used the milk bucket." When I reminded him of this, he answered.

"Vera, you know I didn't do that." I said.

"You really *did!*"

"Otie, you and Ed one night, when I had a date, really embarrassed me. I was sitting in the living room near the stairway with my date. Everything was real quiet and all of a sudden we heard bang, bang, bang, going up the stairs. Every time it went bang it also went ping, ping, ping because the lid on the slop jar would bounce up and down. I was afraid to look at my boyfriend because both of us knew that sound. Finally, Ed reached the top of the stairway and set the slop jar down with a loud bang." Otie was behind Ed going up the steps.

When Ed came back from the Merchant Marines, where he had been one of the chefs, we began talking about different kinds of meat. Someone asked him.

"Is possum good to eat?" He gave his recipe.

"Soak the possum overnight in salt water, drain, put on a baking pan, and roast until it gets tender and golden brown. Afterwards place it on a serving plank, cut fancy carrot flowers, onion rings, green and red pepper rings, and celery sticks. Then eat the plank and throw the possum away."

After this funny story and the family had a big laugh, I stood and said.

"I guess we had better break up while we are still laughing and get the girls home to bed."

My middle daughter, Juanita, was always creating 'adventures' for herself. When she was about 5 years old she and her sister, Janet, decided to play house outside on the terrace beside the garage. So they each balanced themselves on a wheelbarrow so they could reach the window on the garage to wash it. Before long, Janet jumped off her side of the wheel barrow, Juanita flew up in the air, came down and hit the back of her head on a board with a nail. We took her to the doctor and he closed the cut with about 4 stitches. Yes, we bought ice cream for her.

There were at least two adventures involving Juanita driving the new car we had recently bought. She and Shelby Jean were leaving a grocery store parking lot. As Juanita was backing out of the parking space, the front left side of the car caught on a smooth bolt on a truck's bumper. This left a foot-long dent on the side of the car. An idea came to Juanita on how to tell her dad about the dent. They arrived home safely. As instructed by Juanita, Shelby Jean went into the house first and told her dad that Juanita had really banged up the car. When he came to see the car, he had to look really hard to find the damage. The dent didn't really look that bad once he found what they were talking about. Since Juanita was working at the time, guess who had to pay for the car repair.

Another time, Juanita drove the same car to a school function with Shelby Jean and her friend; I was in the front seat. When we came outside, after the function, there was snow and ice everywhere. With Juanita driving on the main icy and snowy road, the first curve she came to, she slowed down and glided the car into a ditch. There we sat! The car's right side was in the ditch and we couldn't get out. As Juanita was too nervous to continue driving, I got behind the wheel. Miraculously, the next car that came around the curve had several young boys as passengers. They stopped to help and before we knew it, they lifted the car out of the ditch. Thank God for those young guys. We were so glad they came along to help us. It could have been devastating.

In September 1956-57 Janet became a senior and Juanita entered her sophomore year of high school.

The first time I met Ray, I thought, he has the most beautiful smile and an expression of love on his face and a quiet spirit. Janet and Ray went to school together from the third grade to the senior year and then graduated together. They married two years later in April of '59. They have now been married for fifty four years. They have two daughters and three grandsons.

Two years before Janet graduated from high school, during the girls' summer vacation, we attended the church youth camp held at Glenwood Park. I cooked for those two summers for the campers, with the assistance of one person. I made biscuits, gravy, fried eggs, sausage, bacon, chicken and dumplings, cabbage, corn, green beans and a large pot of pinto beans with a ham hock for about two hundred people. The Director of the camp brought a half bushel of onions in the kitchen and told me.

"Peel and prepare these onions for dinner. While all adults and children had gone to the City Park pool to swim, I made creamed onions for dinner.

Afterwards, I heard a commotion and saw an ambulance was bringing Sister Scott to her room. I learned later that Sister Scott thought she was jumping into the shallow end of City Park pool. However, she had jumped into eight feet of water and almost drowned. Another thing happened to Sister Scott. She had just pulled her dress off to get in bed, when two girls grabbed her and drug her about twenty feet across to the shower house. Wringing wet, she returned to her cabin embarrassed and was worried whether any of the men saw her returning to her room.

I first met Sister Scott, Pastor of a Church in the coal fields at the 4-H camp in Glenwood Park. A couple of years later, Sister Scott called to ask me to hold a revival in her church, which was twenty two miles away.

Sunday, the first night of the revival, a lady came to the altar to accept salvation. She got up and gave a testimony.

"I went back into sin after I was saved. After coming back to the altar tonight, I am now happier than before."

The revival continued Monday through Thursday night. I put on a dress that I thought was too low in the front. I put a little horseshoe pin at the neck. That night Sister Scott invited us over to her house after church. Not suspecting anything might be wrong, we went. There were two people there that had complained to Sister Scott about the pin on my dress. Sister Scott kept looking down at my pin as she made the comment.

"Sister Reed, we don't believe in any kind of worldliness." I responded.

"Neither do I." Then Harold and I excused ourselves by saying we have twenty-two miles to go and its getting late."

The next day Sister Scott's husband rang the doorbell. When I went to the door, to my surprise, there stood Brother Scott. Since my three girls were in the living room, I invited him in the house. He looked straight at me and said in a harsh voice.

"Sister Reed, do you cut your hair?" Surprised, I finally found the words to answer.

"Yes, I cut my hair and go to the beauty shop for perms." He turned to go and told me.

"We'll see you tonight." I answered.

"We'll be there." I felt the joy of the Lord in my soul. *I thought, how sad, he has been brainwashed to think that religion is a set of rules, instead of a relationship with Jesus.*

After he left I went straight to my Bible, looked up Scriptures on love and knew the Lord had just given me my sermon for that night.

After Harold got home from work, we ate dinner; and he got dressed for the revival. Once the service began, my girls sung their song as usual, and I began my sermon on love. At the end of the sermon, I gave an altar call and people came to pray. Afterwards, I told the congregation.

"Tonight is the last night of this revival. I don't enjoy speaking to a critical congregation and sat down." A sister stood up and shared.

"I was hoping the revival would last longer."

There was turmoil in our country in the sixties, November 22, 1963, President John F. Kennedy while riding in a convertible limousine during a motorcade in Dallas, he was shot and killed by Lee Harvey Oswald. When President Kennedy began his campaign, he inspired the youth in America and now this act of violence didn't inspire confidence for our young people in America.

Jean and I had been to town grocery shopping. On our way home my daughter turned the radio on in the car. When we heard the news, we shared it with two men working on the carport.

"We just heard that President Kennedy has been shot." They were in a state of shock, just like we were. One of the men told us.

"Oh, I wish I hadn't said what I did to my friend, that the President should be shot."

Jean and I went on into the house and sat by the television to learn more of the tragedy. We felt so sorry for his family.

As the country grieved the death of our President, I was glad that I had cut the revival short. I was concerned with a situation between my daughter, Jean, and a young man, Junior, who was the son of trouble makers in that church.

My main objection to Junior was, he drove his car up and down our street trying to get Shelby Jean's attention. Also, he would be waiting for her when she got out of high school. Instead of getting on the bus, she would let him drive her home. One day, unknown to me, my daughter had lost interest in Junior for a Bill, a football player in high school and broke off with Junior. Junior and his mother attended my church one Sunday night. After the service, the pastor told me that someone wanted to speak to me in the foyer. When I entered the foyer, there stood Junior and his mother. The first thing, very hostile, the mother said to me.

"You better get after your daughter; when Junior went down to pick her up at the high school she was wearing lipstick." Our pastor was standing behind her with a big smile on his face. I felt like laughing. I replied.

"If she never does anything worse than wear lipstick, she will be perfect."

Jean began having a strange little cough and her neck was swollen. The choir director told her.

"It's probably because we've had practice so much for the festival in Charlottesville, Virginia." She was to represent Narrows high school as a soprano singer.

After returning from the festival, Jean began having some symptoms as Grandma Morgan. She had shortness of breath, chocking, coughing and gaining weight and the swelling of her neck caused hardness. I took Jean to Doctor Weir at the Bluefield Clinic. The doctor told me.

"Your daughter has an over active thyroid condition." We left the doctor's office with a prescription for thyroid pills. Jean took the pills for one year, while the symptoms continually worsened and I took her back to the doctor. He informed me that the only thing he could do was surgery. He wanted me to call for an appointment during the Christmas holidays so she wouldn't have to miss so much of the senior year of high school. I told my daughter.

"You know how the Lord has been healing family members and he can heal a goiter." Also, I advised my daughter to read Scriptures on healing and we'll have the church and family praying for your healing. I said.

"Shelby Jean that decision for surgery has to be your choice. I will not tell you to do it." A person at church gave Jean a book to read. I could hear her coughing as she read the book. The family attended the West Virginia Camp Meeting at Beckley, West Virginia. Jean went to the altar and was prayed for by the night speaker. We thought sure she would be healed For the next month, Jean's symptoms had gotten worse, and the goiter kept growing. I had been to a healing campaign in Huntington, West Virginia, where they prayed for the sick the year before.

However, when we began watching a television show on Sunday morning, before the fourth of July in 1964, the pictures of people that had been healed at the campaign in Huntington were being shown. Suddenly, there was a picture of a woman with a huge goiter on her neck that I had seen get healed in Huntington. I watched as the man stretched forth his hand, touched that goiter, and like the air coming out of a balloon, the goiter disappeared immediately. As my daughter watched the rerun of that goiter disappearing on television, she and I were thinking. *If God can heal that woman, He can heal me.*

When she turned, Jean saw me worshiping God. She decided not to tell me, until I saw the goiter had disappeared. Instead, we both got up and went to our rooms to continue getting dressed for Sunday school. Not until the fourth of July would I notice that Jean's goiter had disappeared.

A couple from the church, and Bill, were sitting around the big round kitchen table with Harold, Jean and me. Jean was sitting opposite me and for the first time, I saw her neck was normal. I reached out and touched her soft neck and the swelling was all gone. Jean looked at me and smiled. I asked.

"What happened to that goiter?" Jean replied.

"Mother I have been wondering when you would see the goiter is gone." I asked.

"What happened to it?" Jean said. "Last Sunday morning when the man reached out and prayed for the woman's goiter, I swallowed and I felt the goiter go down."

Another day shortly after that, I was working in the kitchen and the girls were on the back porch rocking in the chairs and watching the cats playing. Suddenly the screen door opened and Shelby Jean ran to me with tears in her eyes and said.

"Mother will you come and pray for my little kitten. Something is wrong with her." I thought. *Pray for a cat! We've got 17 cats and I want to get rid of most of them, but the girls did not want to let any of them go and they named each one of them. They loved watching them play in the yard and the cats did keep the rodent population thinned out.*

As I followed Shelby Jean to where the cute little kitten named Tiny laid, she looked as if she was about to draw her last breath. I prayed to myself at first telling the Lord how my children loved this tiny little cat because it was the runt of the litter and it was breaking their hearts for the cat to suffer. I looked at it and at the neck where I noticed a hole around the throat area. I said, Lord help me to know what to do for this little animal. All of a sudden I saw what looked like a worm stick his head up through the hole and disappear again. *The thought came to me to go and get some peroxide and pour it on the cat's neck where the hole was.* I then could see that worm coming more to the surface and I went and got a pair of tweezers and pulled it out. Needless to say, the cat got well and I felt happy that God cares about the simple things in our life also and that He had given me the know how to help the kitten.

The year after Jean graduated from high school, she was lying on a cot in the backyard sunbathing for when she goes to summer youth camp. When I went out to see about her, Jean was asleep. I had forgotten about her being out there. I woke her up! She had a bad sunburn on her chest. I rubbed ointment on her. *I thought. God has healed Jean and he could heal the sunburn.* I called my pastor. Bill had a date with Jean that evening. He joined the family in the bedroom as our pastor arrived. In compassion for Jean, the pastor began to pray. The burning stopped. The next morning, as I sat in church watching Jean direct the choir, I knew she had been healed from the dangerous sunburn. Jean had other young men interested in her. However, the first time Bill came to visit our family, Harold shook hands with him and Bill asked him.

"Do you know that my father was a bootlegger?" I didn't understand the joke between Harold and Bill, when my husband just laughed. Since I was in the kitchen frying bacon and eggs for sandwiches for dinner, I invited Bill to share with us.

After that first meeting, Bill would drive the twenty miles to sit in church with Shelby Jean. Now that Janet and Juanita were married I dreaded to think of losing my last daughter. Janet married her high school sweetheart and Juanita had married a guy she met at Lee University. With all the activity going on around our home, *I began recalling when I was a girl at home at Wilcoe. I remembered one time, my sister and I asked Mother.*

"Is it all right if we go and visit Ruth?" My mother told us.

"Now, come back in one hour." I wanted to go play in Ruth's playhouse under the big tree. The wooden playhouse, built by her two older brothers, was high enough for us to walk around inside. She also had a child-size table and chair. Of course, the hour flew by quickly and Ruth's mother never remembered to tell us when our hour was up. We stayed two hours instead of the one. When we arrived home, our mother had canned a bushel of peaches. We asked Mother where she got them. She told us that a man came by right after we left, selling peaches. In that two hours Mother had skinned the peaches, sterilized jars, and cooked and sealed them. My mother was a fast worker. She loved to can and cook. A month later, Mother told Lena and me. "Tonight you are going to spend the night with Ruth." This news shocked us. I was ten years old and Lena would be nine in the fall. We had never spent the night away from our parents. However, we had a grand time at Ruth's home and when we arrived back home the next morning, we had a new little baby brother. Ed was born at home and now our family consisted of two boys and four girls. For the first time, I wondered how my mother felt when all her children began leaving home, especially, when I secretly got married. I wondered how she felt about her oldest daughter eloping.

When Bill and Shelby Jean had differences of opinions, they parted as friends and I relaxed from worrying that they might runaway and get married.

After Bill graduated from high school, he worked as a boiler maker in Waynesboro, Virginia, and I was proud of Shelby Jean being the choir director at our church.

One Sunday after she directed the choir she went to the back of the church where, unknown to us, she was waiting for Bill. After Harold and I came out of the choir we sat with our backs to her and we did not know Bill was there. What we learned later, that Sunday morning they were planning their elopement. Shelby Jean and her friend had been talking about the elopement on the telephone party line!

The day of the elopement, I gave my daughter permission to spend her first night with her friend. Sunday morning, when Shelby Jean didn't arrive to direct the choir, I assumed she and her friend had overslept. However, when services were over, Harold went to get the car, while many of the church women stood by me without talking. I waited, in case Shelby Jean had been in church and I hadn't seen her. As Harold parked our car, he ran up the steps and just before he started to whisper in my ear, I saw Bill's car parked up the street with clothing hanging in the window. My husband was whispering to me. "They are married." Not one of my friends said a word. Everyone knew it from the party line that they were eloping and kept it from me. I began having trouble breathing. My husband drove me home in silence. When we got out of our car, Bill and my married daughter were getting out of their car. They followed us home. Shelby Jean had come home and gotten her clothes while we were in church. She didn't come in the house. She told me.

"Mother, we have a place to live in Waynesboro."

As fate would have it, that afternoon at five thirty, I had contracted with the radio station to begin a 30 minute broadcast every Sunday afternoon. *I thought my daughter and her two friends were going to sing.* Suddenly, I got the idea to call the church parsonage.

"Would the evangelist pray and your wife and her two sisters sing on my radio broadcast today?" When they all agreed to meet us at the station, everything went well.

After a few more broadcasts, I stopped at the A&P store and after shopping, I checked out with the same cashier I had become friends with. She surprised me when she made the comment.

"I heard your broadcast yesterday evening and I really enjoyed it." I stuttered.

"Sure enough?" I guess there isn't too many people listens to us."

"What?" She replied. "Your program is on even in the funeral home." I told her how that encouraged me to know there are people listening.

That evening when I told Harold what she said, he said.

"That encourages me, also."

March 1965, the American people were very discouraged when our President, Lyndon Johnson ordered the first American ground troops in Vietnam. This was a conflict that had been between the North and South Vietnam for years. This had been a long standing struggle against the Nationalist forces who were attempting to unify the country of Vietnam with a Communist government. Therefore, the United States joined South Vietnam engaged in a war to prevent the spread of Communist and the American people viewed the conflict different from the politicians. There was no way the United States could win because the American troops were fighting a jungle war. The well trained Viet Cong ambushed and tricked our troops by using underground tunnels. Therefore American troops couldn't even find the enemy they were supposed to be fighting. The atmosphere in America became more discouraging as families gathered once again around their radio to hear the evening war news. We learned of our troops dropping Agent Orange and napalm bombs to help clear a way through the jungle in an effort to find the enemy. In the different villages our troops found it difficult to trust any of the villagers because some of the women and children had been trained to build booby traps.

These conditions caused our troops to be frustrated in a no-win situation in Vietnam plus the low morale caused many American soldiers to be angry and drugs became popular. April 30, 1975, the Vietnam War ended and our dishearten troops came home without the support of their efforts from the public, which added to the troops anger even to today. February 9, 1964, before the Vietnam War ended, there were 500,000 young people congregated on the Yasgur's dairy farm and our young people's way of life changed. Ed Sullivan introduced four singers on his show for the first time in America: The Beatles: John Lennon, Paul McCartney George Harrison and Ringo Starr. When the four musicians arrived in New York, at least 5000 screaming fans welcomed the music group to the United States. The Ed Sullivan show pushed the Beatles popularity to an all-time high, which shapes our lifestyle of today. They shaped not only our music but changed an entire generation of people discouraged from the news of the Vietnam War. Instead of wearing the popular 'Missing in action bracelets', thousands impersonated the popular Beatles with their haircuts, clothing, morals and religious beliefs. Around 1966 the Beatle group, weary of their popularity, became known for their psychedelic influences by introducing a new recording, Sgt. Pepper Album and their use of marijuana and LSD plus introducing Eastern religions, which effects the behavior of youth in schools and at home even in the twenty-first Century. Right on the heels of the successful group from Britain, the 1960s young and old lived through shocking events.

August 28, 1963, Dr. Martin Luther King, Jr, delivered his famous, 'I Have a Dream Speech', in the Civil Rights march on Washington, DC. April 4, 1968, Dr. King was shot and killed by James Earl Ray at the Lorraine motel in Memphis, Tennessee. Dr. Martin Luther King, fell violently back- wards onto the balcony. The shock of Dr. King's being shot brought a lot of sadness to civil rights.

April 11, 1968 a little after mid-night, the news of Robert F. Kennedy, United States Senator and brother of assassinated President John F. Kennedy, was campaigning to recover his Brother's presidency, when Palestinian Sirhan, Sirhan fired a .22 pistol and shot the Senator Kennedy multiple times leaving him to die in a pool of blood.

During the same period of time, my Father had been in and out of the hospital most of the winter and finally allowed to go home.

Easter Sunday April 1968, about four in the morning, dressing to go to the Easter Sunrise service, I heard the telephone ring. My sister, Lena, gave me the news.

"Vera, Father is gone; he went to Heaven shortly before four this morning." Immediately, I went to my parent's home to comfort Mother and finish telephoning family members of Father's death. Just a few days earlier, Father looked up at Harold and called him 'Elbert,' his deceased older brother. Then just last night Father in his wheel chair looked around at everyone, and said.

"I'm ready to go." The family, touched by his words, gathered around him and prayed.

There were many bright spots for Harold and me by way of our weekly half hour radio program. Right after Father died, a woman telephoned and asked me to pray with her husband. When I spoke with him, I asked.

"Do you want me to pray for you to be saved, now?" By the sound of his voice I could tell he was under conviction when he replied.

"Yes, right now." I quoted Scriptures and he repeated the sinner's prayer after me, when suddenly, I heard him say.

"Oh, my burden of sin is gone; I'm saved."

The following summer, Harold and I drove to Maryland to visit our oldest daughter and her husband. A day or two later, I called back home to ask Lena.

"How is Mother?" Lena told me, our niece is in John Hopkins Hospital in Baltimore and had been operated on for abscess on the brain; she would be facing another operation in a few days. I telephoned her in the hospital and asked about her having another operation and she told me.

"Yes and I'm scared."

"Do you feel like you're ready to meet the Lord?"

"No, that's why I'm afraid." I knew she was raised in church and for that reason I assumed she was a Christian. So I continued.

"You realize we're all born in sin and that's why Jesus died for us?"

"Yes."

"I will pray the sinner's prayer and I want you to repeat it after me and the Lord will save you." She prayed and suddenly she took a deep breath.

"Oh, I feel so relieved like never before."

A few months later, after the surgery, the Lord called her to her new home in Heaven.

The joy I had concerning my niece, the Lord repeated the morning I awoke thinking about my husband's blinded Aunt Lula. I was impressed to go visit her. She lived about six miles away and I didn't want to drive that alone. I stopped and asked a pastor's wife if she would go with me. She shared that she had started heating water to do laundry when the Lord impressed her mind to change her clothing. She added.

"I wasn't surprised to see you because I knew I would be going somewhere."

When we arrived at Aunt Lula's house, she requested us to pray for her. I told her.

"We will pray that the Lord will heal your blindness." Before the pastor's wife began praying, she gave testimony of how the

Lord healed her son when he was at the point of death. After a time of praying, Aunt Lula said.

"Oh, how I miss worship service. I have family and neighbors that won't go in a church." Mary and I organized a Sunday afternoon worship service for the next Sunday afternoons. Mary's husband, who was a pastor, agreed to bring the message. Sure enough, most Sunday afternoons there were family and neighbors to listen to the Reed Sisters sing and a sermon from the Word of God. We had a time of prayer and the pastor's message. After three or four Sundays, the pastor anointed Aunt Lula with oil and prayed for her as usual. After the church service, I walked towards our car. The words came into my mind. "You forgot something." I couldn't understand. The next morning, the same words came in my mind as I prayed; I asked the Lord.

"What did I forget?" The Lord answered.

"You forgot to raise her up." If that was God, I was going to raise Aunt Lula up the next time. The pastor anointed Aunt Lula and I asked her.

"Has the Lord ever failed you?" She replied.

"Never!" I added.

"I believe when you put your feet on the floor you will be able to walk." She interrupted.

"I am too weak to raise myself up. I asked nearby women to help Aunt Lula to raise up. When they helped get her on her feet, I told her.

"When you stand up the Power of God will come upon you and you will receive strength." Someone brought her a robe and shoes for her feet and then she stood and danced all the way into the living room. The next Sunday meeting, she told us.

"God impressed me to stand up and look out at a family's house and she told God. "I'm blind. What good will it do for me to go to the door." Immediately, she knew if she had obeyed, God would have healed her blindness.

Chapter 8

Our next ministry appeared when Bill and Jean moved from Waynesboro to Glen Lyn near our home. Not long afterwards, Bill got his foot caught in a machine and couldn't work and my husband invited the newlyweds to stay with us until Bill could work again. Once they moved on to a new job, Harold and I began looking forward to more grandchildren.

The Lord blessed Jean and Bill with three special children. One week their little Holley came to visit me for a week. She liked to ride her tricycle up and down the driveway. One day she discovered a sandbox the construction workers had left. There she found a Frisbee and later I found her washing the sand off the Frisbee in the sink. I said.

"Holley, that's not mine. It belongs to some of the neighbor boys." She looks up at me so sweet.

"Grandma, don't you know, 'Losers weepers, finders keepers'.

Then there were the blessing of Janet and Ray's two intelligent girls. Once when visiting them in Maryland, I recorded the next Sunday's radio program on tape with Janet playing the piano. I asked little Rayann a question.

"What do you think of Children's Church?"

"I like it."

"Can you tell me something you learned?"

"Peter, James and John went a 'fis hin' on the deep blue sea."

After four or five months of broadcasting every Sunday afternoon, one day my best friend called me on the telephone.

"My grandson was with a bunch of boys who got into trouble. They were arrested and put in jail. Last Sunday evening the boy in the cell next to my grandson had a transistor radio and he said.

"I'm going to listen to my favorite preacher." When the cellmate turned on the radio, my grandson learned that the preacher was my best friend, Vera Reed. He said, "I love to hear that woman talk."

A friend of mine, from another church, called to say.

"I listen to the radio broadcast with Harold and Vera Reed every Sunday evening. It's just like a drink of cool clear water; I wouldn't miss it for the world."

One night at our church the altar call was given during the revival and Harold's step-father, Gene Morgan, went forward with both hands up in the air surrendering his life to God. When the pastor asked for testimonies, Grandpa Gene shared.

"I know I'm saved because my burden of sin is gone and I thank you for praying for my salvation." After church I said.

"I am rejoicing Grandpa got saved." Nannie, his wife, replied.

"We'll see." She left a partial plug of tobacco in his coveralls and told us.

"If he doesn't chew any more, I'll know he is saved." One day Grandpa, taking his coveralls downstairs for Grandma to wash, found the plug. He took it out of the pocket, lifted the lid on the cook stove and put the plug of tobacco in to burn. Later, when Grandma told me about this, she said.

"When he did that I knew he was saved."

That same spring Grandpa planted a large garden on Kirk Street and his lucky next door neighbor, who was a minister and was a pastor of a church in the coal fields, received all the vegetables he could eat that summer. In fact Grandpa Gene supplied fresh garden vegetables to the neighborhood all summer.

Grandpa became very sick. One day two of the church members passed Grandpa's house and Grandma saw them from the kitchen window. She thought. *Oh, they are coming to visit Grandpa because he is so sick. He had heart failure.* They passed by and went on to visit a widow woman next door and no one from the church ever visited Grandpa Gene. He had become too weak to attend church any longer. Grandpa surprised the family the time he told us.

"This is the third time I have been this weak and this is the last time." Because of the attitude of the pastor, at that time towards Grandpa, he didn't feel free to be baptized or take communion because the pastor had called our family, 'church tramps' from the pulpit.

It began one night when we attended a revival at another church where a longtime family friend was preaching. Also, he had been Grandpa and Nannie's pastor at the church they attended when they lived in Chattanooga, Tennessee.

That winter Grandpa continued to become weaker. One day Nannie called the ambulance to take Grandpa to the Veteran's Hospital in Beckley, West Virginia. Harold and I followed with Nannie in the car. We were thankful that before Grandpa had to go to the hospital that our pastor friend of the family came and administered communion and wanted to baptize Grandpa in the bathtub; but he was just too weak and the pastor sprinkled him in the name of the Father, Son and Holy Ghost.

Once Grandpa got settled in the room at midnight he told us.

"I will be out of here in two weeks." I felt the Lord gave him that message for us. Two weeks later, the hospital telephoned that Grandpa is in a coma." Harold drove me, his sister Naomi, who was visiting from Florida and Nannie to the hospital. When we arrived early that morning, Harold put his hand on Grandpa and prayed. Grandpa's eyes opened and he recognized his stepson. In the middle of the afternoon, Grandpa looked straight up at the wall and said. "Hurry Lord, I want to go." At that moment Nannie and the family gave Grandpa up because he wanted to go. Harold and his mother left to go home and be with our three daughters. Grandpa seemed to be conscious as Naomi and I were sitting in his room and at five minutes before midnight, I saw that he had stopped breathing. I had kept a count of the days since Grandpa had been hospitalized and at midnight it had been exactly two weeks that he had told us, "I will be out of here in two weeks." His neighbor preached Grandpa's funeral and shared how he loved his step-grandchildren and how he loved to help people and all the wonderful vegetables and fruits he grew and shared throughout the neighborhood.

I was happy that I had been there and heard him say. "Hurry Lord, I want to go." I knew he was at rest in the arms of Jesus Christ his Savior.

His neighbors, as well as our family all missed him because he was good to everyone and a good helper in time of need.

My mind goes to a time when Janet was about 5 and Juanita was about 2 ½ years younger. They were playing with their dolls on the patio next to the side of our house, which our neighbor was painting. He was unable to reach the lower wall so he got off of the ladder and placed each foot on the 4" wide arms of Juanita's little chair, which I had made for her and Janet. While painting he reached too far to the right and the chair turned over, causing the paint can to go up and spill white paint on his head. I ran in the house and laughed to myself at the surprised look on his face with paint dripping from his eye lashes. I ran back to him with rags to clean his head and face. Juanita didn't think it was funny. She was busy looking at her little chair wondering if it was ruined and WHY was he standing on her chair? When she finally looked at his face she began to laugh at how funny he looked with white paint dripping down his face.

One of the reasons we moved to Glen Lyn, Virginia, was to be closer to Harold's work. Also our church was in a state of confusion about a lot of things. One day the pastor's wife wanted to talk to me. However, she began talking to me in front of my husband, my three daughters and the pastor.

"You don't accept responsibility in the church. You don't do anything to help us." By the time she finished and Harold drove the family home, he seemed so depressed for the upheaval at our place of worship.

The next Sunday Shelby Jean had her hand on a door and the pastor's daughter slammed the door on my daughter's hand. When Shelby Jean asked her.

"Let my hand loose before you break it;" for a moment, the girl pushed the door harder before letting go. *Jean thought her fingers were broke.*

A few days later, Harold called me from his job at the Appalachian Power in Glen Lyn, Virginia, to tell me.

"Vera, there is a company house coming available. Do you want us to move out of my family home and move closer to my work?" After our pastor called us, 'church tramps' we decided to become just that. We started visiting other churches in Princeton but hadn't found one as of yet. I just told my husband.

"Yes! I think this is God's opening for us to get away from all the confusion."

When Harold took me to look at the house, I liked it because it was close to his job and we already had good friends living in the area. The whole village of company homes stood upon top of a hill.

The spring that we moved to our new house, to our surprise, there was a large Apricot tree in full bloom and when I looked at that unusual tree in our area, I felt like the good Lord had approved our move. The tree was absolutely covered in Apricots. I canned many quarts for our desserts and shared them with the neighbors. The next year there wasn't one apricot bloom on the tree.

When we moved to Glyn Lyn I didn't know that the view from the front of our front porch faced the railroad track where Harold's father, a train engineer for the railroad, had been killed. It was thought that someone sabotaged the track causing the train to derail. My husband was only seven years old when this happened.

We settled into our fresh painted house with our married daughter, whose husband, Ray, was deployed to Korea with the Air Bourne Division of the Army.

Our middle daughter, Juanita, after completing her training to be an Airline Hostess, decided to go to Lee University in Cleveland, Tennessee, to study business. There she sang in the college choir and was a member of the Pioneers for Christ. Also she learned how to transfer playing the piano to playing the organ, and took up playing an accordion.

Therefore, that left our youngest daughter Shelby Jean in high school. The very next Sunday, we attended a church that we had been to before and transferred our membership.

The next day I drove Shelby Jean to the bottom of the hill to catch the school bus to attend Oakvale High School, over the border in West Virginia. In just three days of attending this school, she came home to inform me.

"That school is not for me. There is no order in the classes. I had my lunch money stolen and someone took my sweater that I had left at my desk when I went to the bathroom."

The next day she got on the school bus with the neighborhood children and went to Narrows High School in Virginia. Immediately when the school principal saw my daughter, he laughed and said.

"Here is my country cousin," which made my daughter feel loved and accepted by the students and teachers. Shelby Jean had been taking classical piano lessons and when a student told the choir director. "Shelby Jean plays the piano." The director told her.

"Here is the sheet music. Why don't you play for us while we sing?" My daughter had about five minutes to look over the music with four part harmony plus her accompaniment line. She told me.

"They sang, I played, and today began my experience as NHS choir pianist."

Later, my daughter was chosen to go to District Chorus and also to All State Chorus at the University of Virginia in Charlottesville, Virginia.

By Shelby Jean's senior year at NHS she had been chosen to be a Senior Superlative, as the most talented female in the senior class. She also played the piano and sang 'Moon River' in a variety show. Shelby Jean, and five of her friends, took turns having pajama parties at each one's home. I enjoyed it when Shelby Jean had the girls to our house because I missed cooking for all three of my daughters. One night the girls were staying at Freda's house, where her father would tell ghost stories.

Their favorite had to be, 'The Legendary White Woman'. The story began when the white woman's baby had died and she became so overwrought with grief that she killed herself. Supposedly, she rode around the area on a horse searching for her baby. The legend has it, at certain times one could hear the baby crying. Freda's father told them.

"You can see her, on nights when there is a full moon, in a long white dress with long flowing white hair." Of course, the girls used that as an excuse to go over to Freda's handsome cousin's house that played football at the high school, to look for the 'White Woman'.

One night the girls stayed passed dark and Freda's cousin, Bill Robertson, had to get the tractor and ride them back around the mountain to Freda's house. They were scared in the dark that they might just meet up with the 'White Woman'.

Bill rode on the same bus with Shelby Jean but she couldn't understand him because he would not talk to her on the school bus, just at his home. There were times she would ask him.

"Are you saving this seat?" He wouldn't answer, just scrunched up as close to the window and turned his back. He began calling Shelby Jean a 'snob'.

While still living in Glen Lyn, and going to the church nearby, the President of the Ladies Willing Workers voted to divide the church women in two groups with me as one captain and Elizabeth the other, as a contest, to see which group could raise the most money for the church.

Two of my workers helped me make fried pies for our team to sell. When they arrived at my house I had already prepared the dough and the different kinds of fillings. After frying and selling hundreds of pies, our team made over two hundred dollars. Not only did I have the best fried pies in the state of West Virginia but my husband sold them to the men at the Appalachian Power Plant.

Here is the secret <u>Fried Pie</u> Receipt from the church:

4 cups flour   1 large can evaporated milk
¾ cup shortening(Crisco) 2 eggs (slightly beaten)
¼ cup sugar
4 teaspoons baking soda   2 teaspoons salt

Cream shortening and sugar; add beaten eggs; add flour and milk alternately; dough can be stored in refrigerator and used as needed. Take about 1/3 of cold dough and roll out thin as possible on a floured surface. Lay a large saucer on dough, using a knife to cut a circle, until all dough has been cut. Put pie filling on one side of the circle leaving ½ inch to the edge. Wet the edge of the dough slightly with water and fold over and press the edges together and seal all around with a fork. Then use fork to make one set of holes in top of the pie to let the steam out. Melt about three inches of Crisco in a large electric fryer and heat to 350 degrees before placing one-pie-at-a-time into the Crisco until the fryer is full. Remove the pies when they are golden brown.

<u>Pineapple filling:</u>

Mix ¼ cup sugar 6 Tablespoons cornstarch or flour with enough water until smooth paste. Set aside.

Mix 1 large can crushed pineapple ¾ cup sugar ¾ cup water in a saucepan and bring to a slight boil. Add the cornstarch mixture quickly while stirring vigorously to keep from lumping. When thickened, remove from the heat and let cool and store in refrigerator until time to use. Enjoy!

From the spring of '61 to the fall of '63, we enjoyed living in the company home in Glen Lyn, Virginia. After two years God impressed my husband and me that we should move back to Reed Hill in Princeton and go back to our church.

The spring of '64, the family had a nice surprise when Shelby Jean's friend, Bob, from Narrows came to visit and Bill Robertson was with him. Both Bob and Bill invited my daughter to their prom and she refused them both. As they left, Bill let the family know he would be back the next Sunday. Sure enough when we arrived home from church, there he sat in the car. Their friendship evolved into a courtship and later an elopement.

When we moved back home in '63, we went to our church. After a few weeks passed I wrapped a 'Better Homes Cookbook' as pretty as I could and gave it to the pastor's wife as a love gift. She was pleased and I knew I had forgiven her for the mean way she had treated me. I washed her feet during the next Holy Communion Service and she washed mine and our good Lord blessed us.

After I helped with the youth camp one year, the next project the pastor asked me to fix turkey with stuffing and giblet gravy for the church's Thanksgiving dinner.

The following spring the pastor's wife, 'President of the ladies willing workers group in the church who worked and made money for the church, suggested one way to make money would be to make and sell meringue pies to the workers in the Maiden Form Factory. My part of this fundraiser was to have a couple pies ready every morning when a person from the factory came to my home and picked up the pies. It was a very successful fund raiser for missions. I enjoyed doing any kind of work for the church.

Another ministry of the willing Workers was to take food to families in times of trouble. When someone died I felt like it was my responsibility to take food to the homes when their loved ones died. *After sixty three years of working in the church I wish I could do more work in my church but age takes a toll on our bodies.*

I love to plant flowers and vegetables and watch them grow. I asked Harold to help me plant a large round flower bed in the middle of our front lawn. My husband and I laid out a six foot circle with a water hose in the middle of the lawn. He dug the ground for the flowers to be planted. Then he put a white fifteen inch high fence around that flower bed. Then we went to Broyles Nursery and purchased Coleus and planted them around the edge of the flower bed and then I planned to purchase the tall red flowers for the center of the circle.

The next morning I went down the front steps and turned left and picked up my water hose to water the flowers. When I got close to the flower bed, there were no flowers; they were mowed to the ground. I stood there in shock. It hadn't been twenty-four hours since I planted them and I was glad that I hadn't planted the Forest Fire Celosia yet. I had to believe it was the seventeen rabbits that lived in the woods behind the house, because one day I saw a rabbit standing on the front porch at the head of the steps with a pink Petunia hanging out of the side of his mouth, as if it was a decoration. When I started up the steps, he came down the steps with the flower still in his mouth, passed me up and went up into the garden.

I was so disgusted that I couldn't put out anymore plants in that bed without them being eaten. Suddenly, I had a bright idea from a *'dumb bell'*. I went to town and purchased some Acorn Squash seeds. The pretty green leaves filled the whole bed and against the white fence it made a beautiful scene. This yielded a great harvest of squash, which we gave away and had enough for most of the winter.

I was just remembering when Shelby Jean was about 4 years old, Charlotte, Harold's niece, and her mother were visiting us one Sunday after church. Charlotte got bored and decided to play a joke on everybody. She took Shelby Jean's finger and used it to dial the phone and call the ambulance to our home saying her mother was sick. Then she did the same thing again, but this time she phoned for the fire truck to go to the church parsonage. Charlotte knew she was caught and began blaming Shelby Jean for phoning. I knew Shelby Jean had not been taught yet how to dial the phone.

Then the day came when we saw appraisers out and about our home. One day an appraiser came to tell us.

"There have been three amounts, in three different appraises, on your home." Soon after we were informed that the state highway department was going to take our home and leave us landlocked.

In 1974 after attending a meeting at the Mercer County Courthouse, for the purpose of learning how to settle our home with the state very concerned, Jean asked me.

"Mother have you noticed Father's hand shaking?" I replied. "I haven't noticed his hand shaking but I have seen him dragging his foot and trying to push the mower to mow the lawn. He gave up and came in the house."

After we went to bed that night, I woke to find my husband wasn't in bed. I found Harold standing in the kitchen taking an anti-acid for a burning in his chest. I made an appointment with the doctor. He confirmed Harold had had a heart attack. He spent nine days in the hospital. Afterwards, the doctor's orders were to take three months off from work, rest and get his strength back before starting a walking regimen, no salt diet and get plenty of rest. During this time, we knew that we had to give up our weekly radio program in May of 1975, after almost ten years of radio broadcasting, we gave our farewell sermon. Even after the program went off the air we received many good reports, how God had worked in different people's lives.

After being on radio for several years, a person sent me a beautiful card. In the card she wrote: *"Dear Sister Reed, I'm sending you this card to compliment you on your radio broadcast because you are doing more good then you realize and I look forward to hearing it."* It was a beautiful card, beautiful handwriting and a beautiful message inside. However, no one signed the card.

One Sunday Harold and I wondered if anyone got saved listening to the broadcast. During that afternoon, a man telephones the station to talk to me. He said.

"I was on a drunk the night before your message on the radio. I have lost my wife and family because of being an alcoholic. When I woke up this morning with a hangover, I was thinking about the loss of my family. I turned the radio on, looking for something to help me. After listening all afternoon to many church programs, no one had anything to make me feel better until your program. The good singing and your sermon caught my attention; I prayed the sinner's prayer with you."

One Sunday I asked my father to give the sermon for that Sunday and Harold and I sang before he preached.

One morning, my husband looking in the mirror shaving, he announced.

"You know what? We need to buy a lot in Quail Valley."

"How do you know about that?" I asked. He called back.

"I saw the newspaper ads."

I was looking through my Bible one day and came across some writing that I realized my oldest daughter had put in my Bible as her testimony after she received the Baptism of the Holy Ghost according to Acts 2:4. *I can remember when we came home that night after this precious Gift was given to her by God, she was so happy and she asked me.*

"Mother, if I go to bed will this wonderful feeling leave me?" I told her.

"No, the feeling will stay right with you because that was God and we just have to keep talking to Him. He loves to hear from us all the time."

I copied this from my Bible, where she wrote it when she was thirteen years old:

The Judgment of the Believer's Sin. John 12:31-32

First – Who is the believer? The believer as to sin. Hebrews 9:25-28

Christ died for all our sins. When we are saved our sins are gone. When we become sanctified we are made pure and whole in the sight of God, but if you are holding onto things of this world then you are not sanctified and if you have sin how can you be filled with the Spirit? I say God will not give His power to a person who is not ready for it.

It used to be that when I was little and I would go to the table and pass my plate, Mother would give me as much to eat as she thought I could hold. I would start eating and look around at a good cake or pie she had and I'd think. *Well I want to save plenty of room for that.* So I would look at my plate and I didn't like salad and that was the very thing I should have ate, but I left it. When I finished eating everything but that, I would say.

"Mother, I am ready for dessert." My mouth would really be watering. She'd look at my plate and say.

"You aren't ready yet. You haven't even touched the things you ought to eat. You are not going to get dessert until you clean your plate. I would get mad and say.

"I'm just not going to eat that. When the dessert was passed around everyone got some but me. You know why? I wasn't ready for it. Mother had told me what I'd better do but I didn't do it. If I had obeyed her I would be given the dessert. That is the same way with God. Your heart has to be cleaned out and pure before you get the dessert that God would have for you.

I love to remember the times when we lived out on Reed Hill and the kids were little, we would have such deep snows. They would drift so high in our lane that Harold had to park the car at the foot of the hill and we would walk up to our home.

The next day Harold and I would get dressed as warm as possible and take our snow shovels and reach way up and pull the snow down. Harold said.

"That is the highest snow drift I have ever seen." I said.

"I feel the same way. That beats all."

The coal truck driver told us we could have enough coal hauled in the fall to last all winter and pay for it each month without paying any interest. That helped out a lot. We enjoyed the beautiful scenes the snow made. We have several pictures of deep snow.

We had some good friends who retired in Florida. While visiting us the wife said she was sick of so much sunshine and no snow in winter.

They moved back here and we had extra deep snows and cold weather all winter. They moved back to Florida and stayed until the Lord called them to their Heavenly Home, where there is no suffering of any kind.

Shelby Jean's daughter lived on the west coast where winters are mild with no snow. One winter my granddaughter sent me a letter and said.

"Grandma, please send me some snow!" She now lives in the state of Iowa where they have lots of snow and I am sure she is happy now.

I remember one time, when we lived in Wilcoe, Father bought a cow named Red. We already had one named Strawberry. I ask Father to teach me how to milk because I loved to watch the milk hit the bucket and I realized that I could help because he did not have time to milk and work long hours. Mother had 6 children to take care of and I was ten years old. One day I went out to milk and I sat my bucket down and I sat down on a small stool. While milking with both hands, suddenly Red raised her leg and kicked the bucket, half full of milk, over and me with it. I was so angry I leaped up, placed my hand firmly on her hip and shouted in a loud voice. "SAW!" She never kicked me again. Father taught me to do that. He said. "When you take authority like that it puts fear into the cow and she will stand still from then on and she did.

Chapter 9

The best part of the 1960s my husband and I spent two quiet weeks at Myrtle Beach with our three daughters; it was our first time at the ocean. We stayed in a pleasant apartment, which had a long and wide screened-in porch with table and chairs on one end and on the other end four rocking chairs and a couch. Harold never liked to rock, so he took the couch and I rocked!

One afternoon my daughters and I were rocking, when the man across from us came out of the shower house and walked up the steps to his apartment. When he got to the platform in front of his screen door, his shorts dropped to the steps; we nicknamed him, 'Alley oop'.

It was nice not having to answer the telephone or the door. We completely relaxed as a family. Early every morning, Harold went to the beach to enjoy the cool weather, the ocean and fresh sea air. During the day, Harold and I took the girls floating on truck-size inner tubes and he was the only one of us that could swim. One day at the beach Janet said.

"Look at the funny person's feet in the air with his head through the inner tube under water." Her sister replied.

"That is Daddy!"

The nights at the beach reminded me of how beautiful were God's creations. I loved to look up at the sky when I was a child looking to find the Big Dipper, The Little Dipper, Jobs Coffin, and the Milky Way. *Then I would think, God is up there somewhere and I wished I could see Him.* Furthermore, the rest and relaxation at the beach restored our mental health and confidence in our fellowman to go home and begin again.

～

Many ways the decade of 1970s, started where the difficulties of the 1960s ended; Max Yasgur's fellow neighbors sued him for thirty-five thousand dollars to cover the damages done to their farms, when he allowed thousands of young people to have a rock concert on his dairy farm known as Woodstock. There were still plenty of unrests and public protests because the Vietnam Conflict was still continuing. All the white political conservatism fought to save the traditional family where children would have a two-parent home. The early 1970's news broadcasters brought people's emotions to rise and fall with mixtures of reports; protesters marching on college campus against the Vietnam War; racial protest, television no longer could show cigarette commercials; and the thrill of the Apollo 14 astronauts walking on the moon.

～

Around 1930, I was almost sixteen years old when I read an article in the Baltimore American Newspaper predicting that someday a man is going to the moon! Father thought it would never happen, and I believed the same. My Father died April 1968 and on July 20, 1969, Neil Armstrong's left foot made a print on the moon. At the time, we didn't think technology had progressed enough to put a man on the moon.

On April 12, Easter Sunday, the day my Father died, I was comforted knowing at 60 years of age, he had accepted Jesus Christ as his Savior. Because of Christ's dying on the cross to redeem people, I had hope of seeing my father again. There were many Easter baskets, colored eggs, Easter egg hunts and get-to-gathers down through the years as far back as I can remember. There are pleasant memories of Easter bonnets, new clothes, and Sunrise Services, which my family and I took part in the special Easter programs. Easter is a special time for me because of the celebration of the Resurrection of Jesus Christ our Savior, who arose from the dead, and so will all who die in Christ.

A November day in 1971 my daughter Jean, expecting a baby any day, telephoned me from the hospital in Charleston, West Virginia. She told me of a car accident she and her husband, Bill, had been in the night before. I asked her.

"Do you need my help?" When she replied, "Yes", she began crying. I told Harold.

"I need to get to our daughter." He drove me to Charleston. The doctor had told Jean.

"The accident has delayed the baby's birth." Awakening around five a couple of days later, Bill was getting Jean ready to go to the hospital to have their baby through the Charleston's rush hour traffic. In a hurry, Bill left his billfold at home and late in the day he telephoned to see if I would bring his wallet or some money for food. In the evening rush hour, I found my way through traffic to the hospital. The next morning Bill and Jean became the proud parents of a healthy baby girl, Holley. Things settled down for another month. The week after Christmas my mother-in-law and I were going to do some shopping, riding in my new Electra 220 Buick four-door sedan, we went to the mall. After completing our shopping, we started home and it began to rain. I stopped at the stop sign at the crossroads in front of Andy Clark Auto Dealership.

As I went up the hill towards Princeton, on the right side of the road there was a high bank. I saw the front end of a car, which I assumed was parked in a driveway. Just as I got to the parked car, the woman stomped on the gas pedal and suddenly, she shot out in front of me laughing. Naturally I had to hit the brake to keep from hitting her. Immediately, I stomped the brake pedal and the rear end of my car twisted over on the berm in the mud. My car began heading towards a man standing right beside his broken-down car. When I turned my steering wheel that put me back on the wet highway and the car began to slide over the bank, hitting a tree in the middle of my engine. As I watched what was happening, I thought. *"I am going to die."* Then these words came into my mind. *"I won't let you get killed."* I knew that was God speaking to me and peace came to my heart. I took both hands off the steering wheel, put them in my lap, and prayed in the Spirit. When the car hit the tree it twisted the car, which put my side of the door up against the bank. The impact caused the wide heavy arm rest to fly loose and hit me in the back, and my body lifted up off the seat hitting my face on the steering wheel. Once we stopped my mother-in-law said.

"Oh, Vera, I'm dying; I'm finished." Because of the hit from the arm rest, I couldn't move my head to look at my mother-in-law. She was a small thin lady and had been thrown in the floor up under the dash board. By the sound of her voice, I knew that I had to pray for her. The Holy Spirit took over and I prayed to God in tongues. Then I heard a voice say.

"Lady, can you open the door?" When I opened the door it hit the bank. Then he asked.

"Are you all right?" I tried to speak but I was still talking in an unknown language and he thought that I had to be a foreigner. One of the rescue workers got in the back seat, reached up front and unlocked my mother-in-law's side of the door to get us both out of the car.

At the hospital, we learned the extent of my mother-in-law's injures. Both of her legs were broke in two places below the knee and above the ankle; all her ribs were broken and her collar bone.

I stayed in the hospital for thirteen days in shock and when I would wake up, I would fall back to sleep again. Finally, after almost two weeks of visitors and confusing situations, I asked to be released to go home. I wanted to get in a peaceful place to pray for the healing of my mother-in-law.

She was released after spending 50 days in the hospital because her daughter came, from California to set up a hospital bed with trapezes, and she cared for her mother. Eight months later, my husband and I made one of our occasional visits to check on his mother and there she stood on the front porch with a long handle brush in her hand. We could not believe that the porch walls were covered in suds and running down to the floor where she had been scrubbing. Silently, I thanked God for answering prayer for her healing. *Standing there I thought back to the Thanksgiving Day she had invited our family to come and have dinner with her. On the day of the dinner, we got out of bed and sheets of sleet, as if it was rain, were coming down and covering our driveway, porch and steps. To top that off we had a young man Kenny, who was visiting our home from southern California, who had never seen snow and ice. Playing around in the weather, his feet slipped out from under him and his head hit a sharp stone cutting a 1½ inch long gash. We knew he needed stitches, but we couldn't drive off the slick driveway and the traffic on the highway was extra slow and sliding to and fro. With blood running down his head, I suggested. "Let's pray." We all, Ray, Janet, Juanita, Jean and Harold, laid hands on Kenny and we began to pray a desperate prayer of faith for God to heal our guest with my husband praying in tongues.*

Later when we opened our eyes to look at the cut, it had closed up leaving only a red streak. Our house guess never forgot that miracle because in April 1998, he and his wife stopped by our town and visited me; he was still excited about what God had done. Anyway, we didn't miss the Thanksgiving feast because later in the day the sleet stopped, the sun came out and we drove to Kirk Street for a dinner with Harold's family.

After dealing with two tragic accidents in the family, we joined thousands of Americans listening to the Watergate Hearings. June 17, 1972, all anyone could hear on the television or radio was Watergate, for the next six months. Five men from the Committee to reelect President Nixon were arrested breaking and entering into the Democratic National Committee (DNC). Their headquarters at the Watergate Complex, in Washington, DC, gave way to the investigation become known as Watergate. A security guard at the Watergate noticed tape covering the latches on doors in the complex for the purpose of letting the doors close and not lock. The guard removed the tape; an hour later the guard saw tape on the latches again. So, the guard telephoned the police; and when they arrived, five men inside of the DNC headquarters were arrested.

September 15, a grand jury indicted these men on conspiracy, burglary and violation of federal wiretapping laws. July 1973, as evidence mounted against President Nixon an investigation conducted by the Senate Watergate Committee discovered there were many recordings of conversations, which the President's tape helped to, implicate him. On August 9, 1974, facing impeachment in the House of Representatives and talk of a conviction in the Senate, President Nixon resigned his presidency leaving his successor, Gerald Ford, as President of the United States. Many people around the country feared President Nixon might have a heart attack or even try suicide because of the pressure.

October 1976, after my husband recovered from a heart attack, the doctor recommended that I take him to Charlottesville, Virginia's University Hospital for heart tests. The tests showed blockage, but not enough to warrant surgery. During the four days of extensive testing, results revealed Harold had Parkinson's disease. The doctor gave him prescriptions, which made him very ill with horrible headaches. Next, I took him to Princeton and Bluefield hospitals to be checked with a brain scan. These doctors gave him more prescriptions for his disease and he grew worse. In 1983, after seven years of suffering, our oldest daughter Janet, not only accompanied us but arranged a flight from Washington, DC to the City of Faith in Tulsa, Oklahoma. There the staff believed in mixing prayer with medication plus the hospital had the latest diagnostic equipment.

My husband began to relax in the atmosphere of prayer for his recovery and he began walking around the hospital.

After we returned home, he began driving our vehicles again. However, there were still pressures, from the State of West Virginia highway department, to take our home, which had added to my husband's heart attack. There is no doubt the fact that my husband passed our former home, Reed Hill, every day on his way to work. He was watching daily the state tearing down our home stick by stick. Finally, at the end, the state workers set fire to our home. Seeing it blazing, also stressed out my husband even more because that was the old home place. There would be no more grand views of the sunrises or sunsets from Reed Hill for him. In 1937 we had moved to Reed Hill, where the walls in the house were painted dark colors. After Harold left for work, I painted the kitchen a light ivory color and the woodwork a bright pastel green to match my Sellers Cabinets. The new linoleum and white and green curtains gave the house a cheerful new facelift.

We loved sharing our home so when our pastor announced that a missionary family from Japan would be holding a week's revival at our church, he continued.

"I need someone to volunteer to open their home, to the husband, wife and two children for the week." No one volunteered! Finally, I stuck my hand up because we had one spare bedroom, plus a couch they could use. The couple was given the bedroom, which had a large picture window to view the town of Princeton and the mountains. From their room every afternoon they had the view of the sunset. After I volunteered to house the family, my three girls and I cleaned the house until there was not one speck of dust. The Heil Family flew to the United State from Japan. They rented a car to travel from church to church raising money for their mission work back in Japan. When the missionaries arrived at our home with their son and daughter, we helped them settle in before dinner. Sunday morning I browned a beef roast on all sides, placed it in a heavy roasting pot and filled it half full of water with a heavy lid with a vent. The pot sat on an electric eye on top of the cooking stove with the thermostat turned to the lowest temperature. Just before leaving for church, I checked the temperature a second time. However, after church the Heil family went on to our house, because I felt I should stop at a market on our way home; I didn't realize why. When I saw the real nice pork chops, I purchased them for one of our meals. Just as we topped our driveway, I saw smoke coming from the opened windows. I knew the missionary family found my roast was smoking. Reverend Heil had grabbed potholders and when his wife opened the back door, he threw the black pot and black roast out in the yard. There is no doubt, since the roast was dry, if it had been a few more minutes the pot would have caught fire. There I stood holding a bag of pork chops ready to replace the roast for dinner.

That night, when we went back to church, the nine of us were sitting clustered together. We kept hearing people sniffing, as if they smelled something bad. Later that night, it finally dawned on us the people in church could smell the burnt odor from our pot roast in our clothing.

Missionary Heil preached a week's revival. One night Mrs. Heil dressed in their custom kimono and soft shoes. She explained the weather forecast in her country. When a man put on one shirt, that was called one shirt weather. If it was cooler, the man adds another shirt and that would be two shirt weather or three shirt weather, if colder. Their main staple in Japan was rice, yet I made them mashed potatoes and gravy and the guests enjoyed our ordinary meals. Their two children were so quiet and well-mannered that we hardly knew they were around. If it hadn't been for that burned pot roast, it would have been a perfect week.

Afterwards, we experienced a perfect Christmas, which taught our family and the church family the real Spirit of Christmas. One night my family and I joined the church group going Christmas caroling and had heard the sad news of Mr. Snider's little daughter dying of Bright disease. We went to the house and sang 'Joy to the World' and when the sick daughter heard us sing, she thought that it was angels singing to her. Mr. Snider thought it was the most beautiful singing he had ever heard and invited us into their home. Just a few days later, Mr. Snider asked our Pastor to conduct his daughter's funeral; and the carolers sang at his daughter's funeral. I rejoice, knowing I am on my way to Heaven because of Christ my Savior; I pray continually for lost souls to believe in Jesus. In my spiritual life, I thought I had peace and joy in my heart and had learned to lean on God and to trust Him in times of trouble. Intellectually, I knew all of mankind was born with the instinct to struggle and fight to have their way when all the time God had a perfect plan to grow us up through hardships to be like His Son. Jesus did tell us. *"I am come that you might have life and have it more abundantly."* John 10:10

Well the time came when Harold and I were to be tested to take our hands off many situations and trust God completely. First, we found it difficult to turn it over to God when the State had sent us a letter that they were going to buy our house and it would be landlocked. When Harold's two brothers-in-law heard that the state had taken our home for a highway, they took pity on our situation and contracted to construct a four bedroom, ranch-style house for us.

Not only could I not relax and trust God for the reason our dearly beloved 'Reed Hill' had to go for a highway, but I wasn't happy with our new home! The ranch house was entirely different from the blueprints that I had ordered for a two story colonial house. Because of being in our sixties and my husband's illness, we voted for a ranch-style house without steps. I didn't want to move in the ranch house and my heart wasn't in it. I made the best I could of a bad situation with a selfish attitude.

On top of losing control of our lives, December 13, 1976, after moving into the new house, my sister, Lena, telephoned to tell me that our almost eighty year old Mother had fallen and was in the hospital.

At four o'clock in the morning Mother heard a screen on her rolled out window flopping in the wind and it was sleeting and snowing. However, when she stepped out on the front porch, the wind blew the door shut, and locked her out. Here she was, early morning with deep snow and ice on her steps and driveway and locked out of her house. Stranded she, the 'independent Mother,' decided to go to her neighbor's house for support. She made it down two steps before falling and cutting her head on a sharp piece of charm stone. In order to get to her neighbor's house, she had to cross through a field. When the neighbor saw her with a blood-covered head, she thought. *"My neighbor has been knocked in the head."* Mrs. Cecil cleaned off mother's head, took her to the emergency room, and called Lena. I hurried trying to find my clothes since we'd just moved; when Lena called again wanting to know why I had not gotten to the hospital. When I arrived, Mother started saying.

"I want to go home." She couldn't be home alone with the concussion and I replied. "Mother, you need to go home with me." Once I had her in my home and in a nice warm bed, she relaxed and went to sleep.

A couple of days later, Mother was determined to go home; what an independent woman. After being with my mother, I looked at our modern home in one of the finest subdivisions in the area, and *I thought back to the home of my childhood with Mother and Father*. In the coal fields, where I grew up two families lived in the same house, such as a modern duplex, which at times had its advantages. After World War I ended, I remembered my parents talking how the crime rate had gone up in our town. For one reason there wasn't enough work for everyone that lived in the area. Also there wasn't enough military help for the soldiers, which had been gassed during the war, and that affected their minds. The crime rate increased until the men in the mines decided they needed to put a gun in their homes for protection. One evening Father hadn't arrived home yet from work when someone knocked on our door. It was already dark outside when mother opened the door, and there stood a large-size man staring down at her. She was overcome by fear, still she thought to turn around, and pretend her husband was home. She called out.

"Otie there's someone at the door to see you." The man turned and ran down the street. After that incident Father came home with Yale locks for the doors, braced the windows so they couldn't be raised, and with iron bars he braced the doors so no one could break them down.

When I was 16, the worse scare for the family was one night it began raining and our slate roof directed rain down onto our windows. Mother quietly got out of bed trying not to wake our exhausted daddy, who had come home early. After closing the window she accidentally kicked a shoe up against the wall, making a loud noise. Immediately she heard, what sounded like, two sets of heavy boots running down the steps. Mother woke me when I heard her lightly pecking on the bedroom wall and in a low voice talking to the man in the duplex next to ours.

"Someone has broken in our house. Instead of me going down the steps could you come around back and come through the kitchen?"

By now Father heard the commotion. He got out of bed and by the time he got downstairs, there stood the neighbor man with flashlight in one hand and a gun in the other. Mother went to check on the younger children as they slept through it all. The two men ran out the front door, leaving two sets of black boot prints on the dining room and kitchen linoleum floors. Since Father had been working night shifts, these men didn't know he would be home.

In the beginning of the Great Depression people lost what money they had saved. The stock market crash of 1929 took everyone's money from their bank accounts and any stock they had invested. McDowell county had a place called Gary Hollow, which was a series of towns. Wilcoe was well known as the model mining town of West Virginia. The U S Coal and Coke Company did everything they could to make Wilcoe an attractive place for employees and their families to live. When it was first built, the coke ovens ran through the lower part of town and the heat from the ovens made it miserable to be out and about. Once the coke ovens were no longer needed and closed, the town improved by building fences around the homes and sidewalks. There was even a prize for the three best kept lawns and Father planted all colors of sweet peas, which ran up on strings and covered the rock wall. In the backyard Father planted tall corn along the fence, which helped to hide the neighbor's weeds. In his square flower beds they were outlined with white washed bricks that looked like points in the middle of the green lawn. All around the fence he had planted, nasturtiums and touch-me-nots. In the two beds in the middle he had poppies planted. The tall growing flowers in the middle of the beds, with shorter flowers growing around the edge of our yard, were outstanding. Father won first prize every year. However, during the Depression, jobs were 'as scarce as hen's teeth'. Gary, West Virginia, number 2 mines, where dad worked, closed down. The company divided the work at mines number 6, number 7, and Number 8, with my Father's group of workers. He worked number 8 about a year, and two days before he realized he couldn't continue working part-time without going deep into debt at the company store. When circumstances arranged for him to rent a house in Glenwood Park in Princeton, West Virginia, he moved the family there from Wilcoe.

After my parents set up housekeeping again, Father kept us fed and warm by buying produce from Sterling and Addison and Smith Wholesales in Princeton. Driving back to the coal mines and Bramwell, where people were working, he sold his produce.

President Franklin Roosevelt had great compassion upon the suffering of the people without jobs, money and food. Nevertheless, that didn't stop many people from committing suicide in those days of the Great Depression. My mother used to say.

"My, my, the world is in a bad shape!" *What if she saw it today?* Our country is now in the worst condition it has ever been since the signing of our Constitution. Just as Jesus has warned in the Bible. *"As it was in the days of Noah, so shall it be also in the days of the Son of Man."* From the time I was old enough to attend Sunday school, I wanted to be a Christian. Once I turned twelve years of age, my pastor baptized me and to my disappointment I felt miserable, spiritually. There was an empty place in my heart that I didn't realize that only God could fill. I did not know what to do about this unfulfilled feeling except keep reading my Bible. God dealt with my heart for years, such as when I'd go to a funeral, I got a sick headache and stayed in bed with a severe headache for fear of my death. It would be a period of years before I would come to know God in a personal way by understanding the Crucifixion of Christ was the sacrifice for my sin nature. I guess growing up watching my Father, who had not received Christ as his Savior, read his Bible most every evening after dinner, gave me that desire to know Jesus personally.

Right after I was baptized, Father had gone to the altar but it didn't fulfill his needs. Mother must have understood Father and I had not come to know the truth of the Gospel because the next night she invited the evangelist to have dinner at our home. When Father shared how empty he felt, after going forward in church, the Rev. Bailey replied.

"Brother Lineberry, pray until the bell rings clear." Father and I not only laughed about, 'until the bell rings clear,' but we wondered what he meant.

Finally, 21 years later, after Father turned 60 years of age and I was 33 years old, we found our answer; that we were born with a sin nature.

I couldn't fellowship with a Holy God in my sin nature. Therefore, God sent His only begotten Son to be my sacrifice by shedding His precious blood on the cross of Calvary. Afterwards the bell rang clear and Father realized that many of his family members were Christians before they died. His mother, Adeline Lineberry, died when he was about eleven years old.

Then Grandpa Lineberry remarried a woman whom we called, Grandma Jenny. The newlywed couple had two sons and one daughter, Berlin, Coy and Alma. My Father also had brothers: Elbert, Earl, Jeff and Will and one sister Nettie.

Maybe because Father's mother died when he was young, was the reason that he enjoyed playing with us kids. He loved to gather us around the dining room table to play Dominoes. He was always making us laugh. He had a great sense of humor; everyone liked him. Father would blow up balloons for us to chase and give us boxes of Cracker Jacks and watch our expressions as we pulled out the real toys and jewelry from the boxes. I thought of my maternal grandparents. Even my mother's side of the family were Christians. I had heard for years that Robert and Ebby were devout Christians. Grandpa was 95 years old when he died and Grandma lived until she turned 95 years old.

Now, as I looked at Harold and my new home I comprehended the fact that our home is larger than the little duplex my parents shared with another family. Also, I recognized how my mother must have felt when I and my siblings left home. Once all three of my girls married and had a home of their own, I had to find something to fill my time. I didn't realize I had any talent for art until I found paint-by-number pictures of Blue Boy and Pinky, about 18 x 28 inches. Even to this day the paints are blended so well everyone thinks my oil paintings, framed in beautiful gold frames, are prints.

Next I began making plans to make a home for my grandchildren's visits to grandma and grandpa's house. Less than two weeks after we moved in our new home, Ray and Janet brought our two granddaughters for our first Christmas in the new home. My daughter and her husband brought all kinds of good things to eat and nice presents.

Chapter 10

I love remembering my sixth grade year at school, I memorized a nine page speech about 'Papa's Letter'. It was about a little child talking about her Father fighting in World War I . . . Before time to open Christmas gifts, Father told me.

"I want you to open my gift and wear it tonight." I opened a long beautifully wrapped box, which held the most amazing watch I'd ever seen and I proudly placed it on my arm. Weeks later, I put the box holding my watch upon the mantle; someone crushed the crystal. My father spent a lot of money to mail the watch back to the company and got a new crystal.

After the first of the year, my friend and I prepared to serve a formal breakfast in Home Economics to school officials. Our guests commented.

"The eggs, bacon, toast, juice and coffee were delicious." We received a good grade in Home Economics. To serve that formal meal, I wanted to look my best. I wore my gold watch with the black band. After the delicious breakfast we continued with our school schedule and just before lunch time my watch felt too tight on my wrist. I took it off and laid it on my desk and when the bell rang I ran for the lunch room. On the way, one girl asked. "What time is it Vera?" I turned, ran back up to my room and of course, it wasn't there. I went to the principal's office and told him.

"Someone has taken my watch." After my father finished his meal I told him.

"I hate to tell you this but I lost my watch today at school." I dreaded to hear what he was going to say. When he finally spoke, he looked at me and said.

"I will buy you another one." I figured he just said that to make me feel better. However, the next Christmas he gave me another box to open and there was another watch. Only this time it wasn't gold or as expensive or pretty as the other one but, Father gave me another chance with a watch.

Janet and Ray and their two daughters, Nanette and Rayann, and Harold and I went to Disney World in Orlando, Florida in 1975.

As we came to a theater entrance, the young man taking tickets acted like a robot with his arm stiff with a mechanical movement and his body still and straight. Everyone thought he was a robot but me. I determined to stay until he relaxed. We all went out of sight and ran back, hoping to catch him off guard, but he was still standing stiff and tall. One member of our family said.

"Let's go, he is a robot." I said. "No, he is not." We all went out of sight again. I said.

"I know he is not a robot and I am going to keep on running back until he gives up." Each time I looked at him, I laughed and said.

"He doesn't have me fooled. I know he is a real man." Janet said.

"Mother, let's go. We are wasting time. He is a robot." We went out of sight and stayed longer. I tiptoed back and jumped around the corner and sure enough I caught him moving. We all laughed and he laughed as I pointed a finger at him and said.

"You are a good actor. You had everyone convinced but me." We enjoyed that vacation very much, thanks to Janet and Ray asking us to go with them.

Another amusing incident comes to my mind. Harold and I were visiting Janet and Ray in their home in Maryland. Harold and Ray were sitting on the patio eating grapes and throwing seeds and hulls over in the grass. As the evening wore on and everyone came inside, the scent of grapes drew a small baby possum. Here comes Precious, their small white poodle, and the possum rolled over on his back quickly and played dead. Precious stuck her paw toward him but was afraid to touch him. She finally gave up and went out of sight. The possum jumped up and ran as fast as he could toward a tall tree. Here comes Precious again and the possum rolled over and played dead again. Precious was so puzzled by him so she finally gave up and went out of sight.

The possum came alive again and ran as fast as he could to get closer to the tree. The same thing happened twice more and the possum climbed the tree while Precious just stood there and watched. All my life I had heard the expression 'playing dead like a possum'. I finally saw that expression in action and knew that was the only way a possum could protect himself. I was wishing I had a movie of it all. We laughed a lot as we watched from their dining room window.

After coming back to reality, I knew it was time for my husband to retire from his work. However it wasn't until February 1979 that the progression of his Parkinson disease, with the effects of his stroke and medication causing my husband's walking and talking problems, he made the decision to retire.

After giving up the Foreman's responsibilities he had with his job, he began relaxing around the house and worked in the flower gardens and trimmed faded blooms. He would get on his riding mower and cut the grass. He seemed to really love riding his lawn mower. He was funny in that he always took chances just to see if he could do something that looked impossible. He use to ride his mower on 'Reed Hill'.

One day he started up this hill, which was quite steep, and next thing he knew his machine reared up on him and he had to jump off. Janet hollowed at him. "DAD YOU ALL RIGHT? "He said. "YES, BUT DON'T YOU EVER TRY THAT." He tried this same thing again when we moved to Quail Valley. I came home from shopping one day and the mower was sitting behind the house and it was reared up again. I immediately started looking for him to see if he was all right! I found him sitting in the den. I said.

"Harold, are you hurt?" He said.

"NO, I should have known better." He did not like to fail at anything he tried. He kept the front porch and garage scrubbed clean. As he became weaker, *I thought of the strong man I fell in love with as a young girl. Harold Reed was a self-made man.* He knew what he wanted and went after it with all his heart. He couldn't stand disappointment of any kind. He didn't have any more than an eighth grade education, but he served his four year apprenticeship at the Virginian Railway in Princeton, West Virginia, 1937-1944. He was a quiet man but he had a lot of confidence.

The two years that we lived in Glen Lyn, Virginia, Harold's boss, Mr. Painter, lived next door to us. My husband was a plant supervisor under the leadership of Mr. Painter. He brought a little engine catalog over to Harold and made a suggestion.

"You could order parts from this catalog and you might want to try your hand at building a little engine. It would help you to become acquainted with the machines and learn how to use them."

My husband's personality was quite different from mine. I guess that is why they say, 'opposites attract'. My ability has always been in memorization and the ability to speak in front of people.

I remember at age 18, in l934, I was working at the shirt factory with my sister and two other friends, Enva and Josephine.

They talked me into hitchhiking from Princeton down the old Route 460. The four of us proper young ladies stood on the curve giggling, when a nice lady stopped and picked us up. She let us out of the car opposite the path up the mountain to our friend's, Aunt Jane's house. When we knocked on the door her Aunt opened the door for a surprise; four hungry young ladies. Aunt Jane fried chicken and served it with all the trimmings.

Later, Enva and her Aunt went in the backroom to talk. Suddenly, a dark cloud came up and it looked like it was getting ready to rain. We gathered together our things and bid our hostess goodbye. We walked down the mountain back to a curve to hitchhike back home. By the time we got down to the main highway, it began to sprinkle rain and a man in a pick-up truck stopped for us.

Enva and my sister got in the cab of the truck and Josephine and I were elected to get on the back of the truck. The rain began pouring. The man picked up a tarp and threw it over our heads to keep us dry. As we approached Princeton, Enva asked the man to drop us off at the crossroads since the rain had stopped. We didn't want any of our friends to see us getting off the truck. We had to walk across Thorn Street, the overhead bridge, and through town to the streetcar station.

The next week Josephine, my sister and I, learned why Enva was so anxious to go to her Aunt's house. She and her fiancé wanted to spend their wedding night there at her Aunt's home, since it had been a family tradition for years. The next weekend Enva had a small family wedding at the parsonage and Lena and I were invited to the wedding dinner afterwards at Enva's parents home. While waiting to be invited in to dinner, we asked Enva's little sister where we could get a drink. She led us down the hill to a spring house without anything to dip the water out. I asked. "How do we get water out of the spring?' She replied.

"You just stick your noggin in!" Needless to say, we went back up the hill more thirsty than when we went down the hill. Harold and I married the following spring on May 31, 1935.

After we moved back to our house in Princeton, 1963, we lived there until the highway 460 took our home in 1976. December 13, we moved to Quail Valley.

―⁂―

The second spring, 1978, we planted flower and vegetable gardens. In the month of May, it rained every day and I wondered how I would get my candy corn seed planted, which I had ordered from Guernsey's Seed Catalog. With directions of how to plant the corn, I took a stick that was the length of how far apart to plant the seeds. Then I marked two inches for the depth and stuck it in the ground. After making the two inch holes and adding the seed, I poured dry potting soil in the hole up even with the ground. That year the corn grew way above the roof of the house. It was so tall I couldn't reach the top of the big stalks Later in the summer Juanita and Dennis came to visit and I asked.

"Would you like corn for dinner?" When we walked out the back door to the garden, my daughter enjoyed helping me pick the corn off the stalks. It turned out to be the best corn any of us had ever eaten.

Harold built a kitchen in the garage with wall cabinets over the Frigidaire double oven electric range. He showed me his plans for a free-standing pantry and I asked.

"Will that job be too big considering your health?" He answered.

"It will be a challenge, which I need." He built the frame of the pantry in the basement workshop. Later when I was away from home, he brought the frame up to the garage by himself and finished the pantry. Now that I had another kitchen, I'd go in the garage to fry pies and over the years, I fried hundreds of pineapple, raisin, apple, and peach pies and put them in little sandwich bags. At one time I put 4 dozen in bags for the bake sale for the Ladies Auxiliary to sell at a local bank.

Once Harold had finished the kitchen in the garage, my husband began looking for another project. I showed him another plan for an island in the kitchen that I would like for more storage. Once he finished the cabinet, he went to a cabinet shop for the cabinet maker to make the top for the island. After months of projects, Christmas of 1982, Harold weakened from the Parkinson and needed assistance to function. He shook so badly with the Parkinson that he could barely walk by himself. In the mornings, I helped to get him out of bed and to get him to the bathroom. I bathed and dressed him before feeding him breakfast. Even if he was sick and weak, I was thankful to God that he was still with me. My husband almost died in 1983 and I prayed that the Lord would let him live for our fifty years of marriage. My prayer was more than answered; he lived well past our fifty-fifth anniversary. Harold asked Janet to take me to the mall to purchase something special. When we saw a beautiful fiftieth anniversary ring with 10 diamonds, Janet asked.

"Don't you think that is a beautiful ring?" I told her.

"It is way too expensive." When we returned home, I went to the bathroom and when I returned to my husband's room, he and my daughter were whispering. He wanted us to get him dressed and take him to the mall to see the ring, which he bought for my anniversary gift. April 1, 1984, burglars broke in our home while we were at prayer meeting and stole my wedding band and engagement ring. I thank God that I was wearing my watch with 10 diamonds that my husband gave me on our fifth anniversary, and the 10 diamond fiftieth anniversary ring was on my finger.

I remember my father had given beautiful jewelry to my mother. She was a beautiful young girl growing up in Galax,

Virginia, and she was known for her beauty. Also, Mother made Lena and me the most lovely dresses in growing-up. She made us play clothes to wear skating on the sidewalk, to ride our little red wagon and to play hide-go-seek with the neighborhood children.

In the wintertime, our friends Ruth and Evelyn sat with us in front of the fireplace waiting for chestnuts or potatoes to get done from the hot ashes and we helped Mother make fudge or sea foam candy.

We always had our dolls with us and at Christmas time everyone in town gathered in front of the company store. After a short devotion, Santa gave all the children a box of candy, an orange and apple and all the adults received a calendar. Those were happy carefree times.

However, life wasn't as easy when my husband suffered with Parkinson disease. I felt as if my prayers for his healing weren't getting out of the house.

On May 31, 1985, when Harold and I celebrated our fiftieth wedding anniversary in the church's fellowship hall, they used the church sign to say, 'Happy Fiftieth Anniversary to Harold and Vera Reed.' The room was packed with well-wishers enjoying the refreshments; and Harold and I cut the beautiful wedding cake, which we didn't have when we eloped. Before the celebration I searched until I found Lucile, who went with Harold and me when we eloped. When Lucile was asked to say something, she surprised me, when for the first time I heard a funny story.

"Vera, when you and Harold were going to elope to hide that secret, you told people that you were going to witness my elopement with Barry. The rumor got around town that Barry and I had gotten married. One evening Barry and me were swinging on the front porch and the neighborhood showed up with their noise makers to serenade us.

Just when I didn't think life could get any more out of my control, I had an overwhelming situation that made me turn completely to God. May of 1990, I planned to go to the annual Mother and Daughter Banquet at out church. Even though not one of my three daughters could get off from work I planned to go for the pastor's wife, who insisted on everyone coming to meet her daughters. Once I went to the office to purchase my ten dollar ticket, these words came to my mind.

"Don't go!" I didn't write the check and left to go home. Later, my friend was insisting that I attend the banquet because I was more her age, so for the second time, when I tried to purchase a ticket, the words, *"Don't go!"* went through my mind. After that, I told the pastor's wife that I would not be going to the dinner.

One evening she came to my home, gave me a ticket, and said.

"I really want you to come to the banquet." The day of the banquet, Harold had regained enough energy to be outside, while I prepared to get ready. I set up the ironing board, pressed my new pretty pink dress and made dinner for my husband. Three hours before time to go to the church, I took off my blouse and started to get ready to go. Once I finished, I turned to go and put away the ironing board and cleaned off the kitchen cabinets. From the laundry room I lifted my left foot to step up a good ten inches. Being that I was in a rush, I hadn't lifted my foot high enough and I fell in on the family room floor. I landed on my left shoulder. My arm was twisted out of socket, when the rest of my weight went down, my arm pressed against my body and the sharp elbow broke two ribs. I rolled over on my side and with the aid of my feet I scooted back towards the laundry room trying to set up. I failed at reaching the door knob to pull myself up and finally, I thought. *'The Lord is present in time of need'* and

I prayed, "God, please, let Harold come in the house and not sit down in the garage as usual." In a few seconds my husband opened the door and I shouted.

"HAROLD, I FELL AND BROKE MY ARM! Go in the bedroom and get my robe, and put it around my shoulders."

Afterwards, my husband called Fred, our neighbor, to ask for help. Fred and his grand- daughter, Tina, arrived and she called 911. In a few minutes I was on my way to the emergency room. Doctor Rob operated, putting two metal pins into my shoulder to hold the bones together.

Then the next X-ray showed I had two broken ribs and his nurse put pressure on my ribs to wrap my ribs as tight as possible so they would come together to heal right.

I stayed in the hospital nine days and it was so comforting to see Ray and Janet, when they arrived from Maryland and next Juanita and Dennis came to stay and got me settled in a hospital bed and hired Joyce to come every day to do all the chores.

Early one morning, I went to get my husband out of bed and when I pulled him up with my one good arm, I made a face from the pain in my broken ribs. Harold told me.

"I don't like the look on your face; I am going to replace you." Since I was pulling him up by his left hand, I pulled his wedding ring off, threw it across the room and replied.

"You won't have any trouble getting rid of me." The reason his comment shocked me so much, it was the first time in our fifty years of marriage that he ever said such an unpleasant thing to me.

Finally, I got Harold out of bed into the bathroom and got him dressed. After breakfast, he stayed in the family room the rest of the day. That evening after I fed him his dinner, he asked.

"Where is my ring?" I said.

"Do you want it?' He nodded, yes. I went to the kitchen and got the broom. I went into the bedroom and got down on my knees. I swept his ring out from under the dresser. Cleaning the dust off the ring on my way back to the family room, I put the ring back on my husband's finger as I said.

"When I said my marriage vows, I meant them for life."

Things settled down for a few days. Then I went to help get my husband out of a light weight chair sitting by the fireplace. In trying to help him out of the chair, with my broken arm and broken ribs, somehow he got switched to the wrong side of me. I told him.

"Wait until I get on the other side of you." Just as I stepped behind him, he wheeled around and flung himself back into the light weight chair, which turned backwards and fell to the floor. I heard a bang and didn't know if it was the chair or his head. That was the straw that broke my emotions. I sat down on the couch and cried and cried. Finally, I got control of myself and went to check on Harold. I went over and put his right hand in my right hand as I prayed. *"Jesus help me get my husband up,"* and the chair came up so easy. Then I asked.

"Harold, did you hit your head?" He told me.

"No, I would like to get something to eat.

One morning before he fell, I got him out of bed, took him to the bathroom to get dressed and helped him wash his hands before eating. I guess the most humorous thing that happened during those hard days for the both of us was, the first morning Joyce came to help, I heard Harold calling me. I heard a desperate cry from my husband. He had poured half a bottle of oil into the tub and it was so slick he couldn't get himself out of the tub. I told him.

"Harold, pull the stopper to let the water out and I will help you to get out of the tub." I took the hose and rinsed him and the tub. If you will help me, I will pull you out somehow. I finally got him out of the tub, just as the doorbell rang. It was my sister Lena, coming to visit and see how my husband was doing.

Then finally it came time for me to get my bandage off my shoulder. After a few more weeks my arm was well enough for the pins to come out. I had taken two physical therapy sessions and I was hoping to get more times in therapy to better help Harold, but then he became worse. The ambulance had to be called and he went to the emergency room at the hospital. Harold's heartbeat was so low they could hardly get a pulse. Harold was making sounds but you couldn't understand a word. They took an x-ray and the doctor told us.

"There is a big stone ready to hit and burst the gall bladder." They recommended that we take him to the Richmond hospital. My granddaughter and her husband drove the ambulance that took Harold all the way to Richmond. On the way, Harold became more like himself. He began to want to sang hymns and tell stories to entertain his granddaughter Dawn. Also, I am sure he wanted to get his mind off his situation. In times like this he knew that God was his source and singing was one way to worship Him. He and Dawn sang 'Blessed Assurance' and 'Amazing Grace', which helped to put a positive light on his problems. I was sitting up front in the ambulance praying for him and believing that God would help us through this. When we got to the hospital in Richmond, Virginia, they gave him a liver scan. I was told by the doctors in Richmond they didn't see anything like what they had told us in the hospital in Princeton. Mainly, Harold feared that I might die and leave him, but in fact I was praying for the Lord to let me live to take care of my husband.

The doctors had shared that they had no treatments for my husband's lungs, which were coated with asbestoses; the liver was deteriorated from taking too many heart pills, which slowed down his heart and not enough blood flowing to clean the liver. Also his gall bladder had dried up. The doctor in Richmond sent Harold back to Princeton to rehab because there were no treatments to save him. At noon I went to visit Harold at the rehab.

He was sitting in a pink shirt, without his undershirt, freezing. He had a breathing machine to help him breathe. I stayed the night with him at rehab. He told me.

"I had a bad dream last night." Some men came to take him to the hospital and he began screaming, "Vera, Vera." He got on the elevator and I never heard the rest of the dream.

Monday evening, when my husband was admitted to the hospital, I said.

"Harold just get your mind on Jesus because He is going to raise you up or take you home to be with him. You have the seal of God on your life." The last time I went in his room, I saw my husband looking up for Jesus. His skin felt like parchment paper and I rubbed lotion on him and I felt that I was anointing him for his death. September 19, 1990, my husband had a light that came on his face and the worried look had disappeared. About five minutes after I left his room, my husband breathed his last breath. I saw the nurses heading for his room. I knew the Lord had come for Harold. God gives grace to the widow.

The year that Harold died, Janet called and told me she thought I had grieved enough and she wanted me to come to her home in La Plata, Maryland, for all the holidays for the next two months.

"Mom, I just can't see the family coming to your home and remembering how it has always been, with Dad and you there. It would be so sad for us." I agreed, knowing she was right.

Coming to Janet's home, was a good thing for me, it distracted me from the reminders of what I had just went through.

At that time, Janet was Director of Music at her church. She was planning for her Christmas Program and also, a chance came for her choir to sing at the new mall that was just opening. She ask me to sing in her choir. "Mom, I could use another soprano." I agreed. She had on her program, a piano duet, since one of the stores loaned a grand piano for the occasion and her pastor's wife played for the choir to sing. That was a special time for me in many ways. I loved being with my family members that year.

Since one of Janet's lifelong ambitions was to go to California, she decided to plan a trip for Ray, Janet and myself, to go to California to see my sister-in-law and most of her family members who lived nearby.

Since Harold was gone, I thought I would never be able to see the Pacific Ocean, but there it was! Ray pulled over and parked while we got our fill of looking at that dark blue water. We went driving down the coast. All of a sudden Janet shouted.

"RAY, THE ROAD IS OUT." He said.

"Don't worry! They have given us a detour over toward the bank." Janet said excitedly!

"NO, NO, take me off of this road and away from this route, since it seems to be falling away. How do you know whether or not some of the rest of the road is falling away today, before they can set up a detour?" Find us another road, PLEASE! Ray replied.

"Okay honey, just for you."

We stayed a couple of days in Redding with my niece and her husband. They were happy to see us. We also visited my sister-in-law, who was sick at the time. When she saw us she said.

"You sure have made me feel better, talking and visiting. She also ask Janet to play something. She was always a good piano player herself for many years.

They took her to the hospital while we were there and found out she had low sodium. She was getting better when we left.

We went to see the Redwood trees and that was so interesting. They had made a small house with one window and a door inside of one of the trees so that you could go inside and sit for a minute.

All of a sudden, as I looked at the opening, I saw the backside of Janet coming out and she had white dust on the back of her pants. I started laughing.

"Why in the world are you backing out of there?" She answered.

"It is so tight in here I am thinking, I'd better go out the way I came in." I laughed even more. Then we went to the rented car we were driving and Janet drove it through a redwood tree. It was just a big enough hole to drive one car through. Ray was making a movie of all this.

Next day we drove to Napa Valley, where they have a lot of vineyards and places to go and visit. I thought, how beautiful and clean this place is and I don't see any weeds or bugs. We went inside the winery and Janet was excited about the cherry wood trim for the woodwork and huge shiny stainless steel vats. We were invited to have a glass of wine with some small pieces of bread, which we buttered. This was my first time of tasting wine. I wrinkled my nose because it had such a tart taste. *This caused me to remember that Jesus' first miracle was turning the water into wine. Also, that when He was with his disciples here on earth at the last supper, He told them that He would not partake of the fruit of the vine again until they were together at the Marriage Supper of the Lamb. I got all excited when I thought about I already have my reservation for my next glass of wine on that same day with Jesus. What a time it will be! Being with all of those that have gone before us.*

Then the shock of about the seventh war so far, which I had lived to witness, was announced on television. It was February 28, 1991 was the Gulf War, also known as Operation Desert Storm.

A thirty-four nation's coalition, led by the United States, attack against Iraq because they invaded.

Kuwait. Then Kuwait's invasion by Iraqi brought immediate economic sanctions against Iraq. The United States President,

George H. W. Bush, deployed United States forces into Saudi Arabia and this war was shown on television live from the front lines of fighting. The public became addicted to watching the broadcast of Operation Desert Storm every evening after dinner. Iraq launched Scud missiles, which 'scud' became a new word in every household, against Israel.

April 12, 1992 Mother died. She was born in 1891. Mother had to have a pace maker. Every time we got someone to stay with Mother she would run them off. She would tell us.

"I can live by myself."

My mother, Rose Ella, lived at City View Heights, where she had to go to the basement to put coal in the furnace and we were afraid she would fall.

From the time Father died, Mother told me.

"I want you to get me to a place to be around people." She would even get neighbors to take her to the hospital so she could be around people. The doctors would send her back home because they had no reason to keep her. She was in good physical health except she had hardening of the arteries. Mother had a bad toe nail and Lena and I took her to a foot doctor to have it removed.

The doctor told us that there wasn't enough blood going to her brain and I advise you to get your eighty-seven year old mother in a home. After we entered Mother into Birdmont Nursing Home, and with my husband's illness, I hadn't visited her as often as I wanted to over the twelve years she would be there. Mother sold her property, which my Father had left her to help pay for her stay in the home.

One day Juanita and Dennis came home to go visit my mother at the nursing home. My mother loved seeing her granddaughter. When time came for us to leave, Dennis went out to the car ahead of us. My daughter walked ahead of me through the nurse's station towards the door. Suddenly, my daughter disappeared from my sight, and then I heard her say,

"Mother." There she stood back of the nurses' station with all the nurses laughing. One of the nurses said to my daughter.

"We can't keep clothes on that man." Then I saw the nude man. I told Juanita.

"Let's just walk fast past him and do not look in his direction."

The nurse would take Mother to the shower every morning, and Mother would look up and say.

"Jesus, why don't you just take me home?" The nurse would tell Rosa.

"You don't want to leave us, we love you." Mother's roommate, Lucy, kept us laughing every time we visited Mother. She told funny jokes and recited poems. For her ninety-second birthday, we took Mother gifts. Mother asked me.

"How old am I?' When I told her, 92, she lit up like a light and said, "Oh, I have eight more years to live." The year Mother was to turn 100 years of age, I began early contacting relatives from around Galax, Virginia area to attend Mother's hundredth birthday party.

In the Green Room, at the nursing home, there were over forty people that attended my mother's one-hundredth birthday party. During the party, Mother was sitting in her wheel chair with everyone gathered around her. She looked up with a smile on her face and said.

"Oh, I am enjoying this so much. We should do this more often."

To top off the one-hundredth party, Willard Scott showed Mother's picture on television and announced she had turned one-hundred years young. After twelve years in the nursing home, Mother had not been ill and she wasn't taking any medicine, but at times her mind played tricks on her.

Three months before mother would have turned 101 years old, on April 12, 1992, the nurse took mother to the shower as usual, and she looked up again and said.

"Jesus, why don't you take me on home now?" Mother just bent over the nurse's arms and died, peacefully.

After my mother died, I was left in the world without husband, parents and most of my siblings were gone and I missed the holiday gatherings at my mother's house with lots of talking and laughing.

Days before I turned 99 years old on August 16, 2013, I got out of bed and walked into the kitchen in my night clothes. I began thinking. *What would be good for breakfast with my coffee? Oh yes! My mother's old fashioned buckwheat pancakes with gravy and Father's excellent homemade sausage he made from the best parts of the hog meat and without gristle. It made me homesick to be a child again. However, when I thought about how I suffered standing in that hot kitchen with sweat running down into my eyes and my back churning the sour milk, which Mother let sour overnight, I decided it is nice to live in modern day when I can reach in my freezer and pull out a frozen waffle and heat it in my toaster and add butter and syrup to it.*

This is the way my mother would make the buckwheat cakes. She would put all these ingredients in an old stone crock:

4 cups of fresh sour buttermilk with approximately

3 cups of old fashioned buckwheat flour(mixture should be thin enough to fry)

After mixing these two items, she covered the crock with a plate overnight. The next morning the batter would be full of bubbles and smelled sour. Once she added the teaspoon of soda and mixed all the batter together, Mother would grease a black iron skillet with a meat skin from the fresh killed hog. After that she poured approximately half cup of batter into the hot greased skillet until the cake bubbled on top and then she would flip it over in the skillet.

For Mother's homemade gravy, Father would slice four or five slices of fresh killed hog bacon for Mother to fry until it was crisp; then she would take the bacon out of the bacon grease. To the grease she added enough flour to thicken. This made, what was called, a roux. Then she would fill the skillet half full of milk and stir until the gravy became thick. This bacon gravy tasted so good over buckwheat pancakes with the crisp streaked bacon.

Also the picture of my father sitting at the kitchen table as mother laid a large hot baked sweet potato on his plate. I couldn't take my eyes off his potato as he cut the hot potato down the middle lengthwise and then he took his fingers and mashed each end towards him. As a ten year old girl, I wanted to do my sweet potato as my father did his. However, when I tried for the first time, I burned my fingers on the hot potato, so I sit still until it cooled enough to push it together. Father and I filled our potato with Mother's fresh churned butter, which she made in a one pound printer with a design on top.

These old fashioned menus were real staple foods for large families in times past. After remembering my parents and the good foods from those times, I began looking forward to my family coming in to help me celebrate my 99th birthday.

August 16, 2013, on my 99th birthday, all three of my daughters, Janet, Juanita and Shelby Jean and their families were here at my home and I had company for the whole birthday week. My youngest daughter Shelby Jean and her two daughters, Dawn and Holley, had organized the dinner at a steak house with three or four long tables. There were seventeen people there to eat. First table, I sat with my three daughters and their husbands: Janet and Ray, Juanita and Dennis and Shelby Jean and Bill. At the second table Janet's daughter: Rayann and her husband David; Shelby Jean's two daughters: Dawn and Jim and their two children, Jonathan and Kristin; Holley and Lynn with their two children, Cameron and Katey.

Each one of us ordered what we wanted from the menu. I enjoyed a harvest salad with a variety of greens, berries and nuts with chicken tenders.

While we waited for our food, a man and a woman came in and sat opposite the second table and when the couple got up and came over to hug Shelby Jean and Bill, we were surprised. Later we learned they were distant relatives of Bill. Once I was introduced to the woman, I told her about writing a book of my memories and she told me.

"Oh good! I'd love to have a signed copy of your book."

Another customer in the restaurant came over to introduce herself and wanted to meet me. She said, "You don't know me and I don't know you but I would like to congratulate you on your Birthday." I told her my name and age and she was shocked and replied.

"You don't look 99 years old." I also told her that I was writing a book.

"I'd like to have a copy and have you sign it for me." After talking with the two women, we ate a delicious meal and the staff of the restaurant brought me a complimentary ice cream sundae and gathered around the table to sing happy birthday to me. I enjoyed watching my family singing along while clapping their hands.

Growing up in the 1920s we didn't have radio, television or telephone and in the last almost one hundred years, there has been amazing changes in communication, travel, medical science and the world in general. When I was growing up you never heard of anyone dying of cancer. Life was much simpler back in the early 1900s. We chopped wood, built fire in the cook stove to cook meals. We carried water from a spring, and rode a horse and buggy. However, if I lived like that at my age now, I wouldn't be able to live alone in these days. We were healthier and happier, working out in the fresh air planting gardens, feeding livestock and milking the cows. We never had computer problems, which 1999 caused a world crisis known as the Y2K impact on the new twenty first millennium. I have come from the horse and buggy days to space travel and everything in between.

⌒⌒

In May of 2013 I became ill in my body. I was sore and weak and I couldn't walk because my feet and legs were swollen. Before I became ill, I felt an urgency to write my life story and I prayed, "Lord, put me in contact with someone who would be able to help me write a book." Later when my health worsened, my neighbor, Mary Helen, called the ambulance and they took me to the emergency room. The doctor decided to admit me for a complete check-up. After three days, the tests showed that arthritis caused the problems in my body. When I returned home, I felt helpless as a baby. A lady from church stayed day and night with me until my daughter Janet, arrived from Maryland. Janet spent the whole day on the telephone trying to find someone that could help me on a regular schedule. Finally, in desperation, she called along time friend, Dot George, to see if she knew of anyone. Dot volunteered to telephone some people from two different churches; and everyone had a person they were already working for. When Janet needed to get back home for an appointment, Dot volunteered to stay with me until she could find someone. When Dot came the first day, we got to talking about a book I knew she had written. I begin to ask her questions about her book and I told her. "My children and grandchildren are after me to write a book but I don't have anyone to help me." She said, "I will help you." The next day she brought her equipment, which was strange to me. *I was expecting a typewriter.* As I dictated she wrote on a laptop computer. Then as we completed several pages she e-mailed them to Janet to edit. When the book was finished, Janet brought the manuscript to me to proofread.

During the first few days, I gradually regained my strength enough to walk with a walker and to sit for the long hours of telling my life story to Dot.

To all my family, friends and readers, I hope my life story will inspire you to know how God can reveal Himself to those who seek Him.

Over the years many people have insisted that I write a book of my life. When I gave a talk in Sunday school, the teacher told me that I should write a book. One night at the grocery store a friend introduced me to an editor who attended my church; he wanted to help me write a book. One of my granddaughters put a tape recorder on a table next to my chair so I could record something that happened to me during my childhood. Another granddaughter brought me a journal to fill out, which I'm about finished answering the questions. I pray that this book will inspire you to look back on your life as I have just done by writing this book, and see how God has protected you with his love all your life, and he will never leave you or forsake you.

Vera Reed, 99 years young, August 16, 2013

Vera B. Lineberry

Memories of a 99 Year Old Lady

Harold H. Reed

Acknowledgments

Thanks to Dorothy and Janet for a good job of getting my words on paper. I am thankful to Holley, one of my granddaughters, for giving me a journal containing 200 pages for me to answer questions on each page. This was in 1988, on my 84th birthday. This inspired me to write.

Thanks to Nanette, my oldest granddaughter, for taping some of my stories and also encouraging me to write a book.

Janet Short's husband, Ray, helped Janet with his expert knowledge of the computer. Thank you Ray for all you have done.

Thanks to my Sunday School Teacher, Bob Paitsel and his wife Karen, for encouraging me.

Thanks to my Pastor's wife, Carolyn Hurt.

Many more I'd like to mention but space and time will not permit. I hope this book has been an inspiration to you.